Praise for *Year of the Witch*

"Presenting a fresh take on an old subject, Tempera........ .... *Year of the Witch* has a refreshingly conversational tone. Temperance encourages us to both live in the moment and in the specific environment in which we find ourselves. This book is great for people new to the wheel of the year, as well as old friends seeking to refresh and reinvigorate their practice."

—Amy Blackthorn, author of *Blackthorn's Botanical Magic*,
Sacred Smoke, and *Blackthorn's Botanical Brews*

"*Year of the Witch* surpasses all other wheel-of-the-year books on my shelves as a perfect mix of traditional practices and modern application . . . An absolute 'must-have' if you're looking to incorporate the wheel into your life without the pressure of ideas about what you 'should do' and only build instead upon what is authentic to you."

—Olivia Graves, The Witch of Wanderlust

"Temperance Alden is at the fore of a new generation of witches, and they are smart, fearless, and ready to overthrow paradigms that many of us have taken for granted. *Year of the Witch* invites readers to challenge the assumption that the wheel of the year needs to uphold Arcadian agricultural ideals that just don't apply to how we actually live and practice our Crafts. Temperance is here to remind us that we don't know as much as we think we do, and thank goodness for that."

—Thorn Mooney, author of *Traditional Wicca: A Seeker's Guide*

"Temperance Alden has written a book about the wheel of the year that can finally serve all witches and magickal practitioners living anywhere in the world in any climate. The authenticity in Alden's prose enables her to effectively teach how to develop intuition and work with elements, leading to a more profound understanding of the power of life's cycles. Delightful recipes and engaging rituals and spells help readers to create a wheel of the year unique to their own experiences. *Year of the Witch* is a direct conduit to Mother Earth and all Her power, and Alden has unveiled secrets even experienced witches will want to know."

—Lawren Leo, author of *Horse Magick:Spells and Rituals for Self-Empowerment, Protection, and Prosperity*

YEAR OF THE WITCH

YEAR OF THE WITCH

*Connecting with Nature's Seasons
through Intuitive Magick*

TEMPERANCE ALDEN

WEISER
BOOKS

This edition first published in 2020 by Weiser Books, an imprint of
Red Wheel/Weiser, LLC
With offices at:
65 Parker Street, Suite 7
Newburyport, MA 01950
www.redwheelweiser.com

ISBN: 978-1-57863-712-6
Library of Congress Cataloging-in-Publication Data available upon request.

Cover design by Kathryn Sky-Peck
Interior illustrations by Opia Designs
Interior by Kasandra Cook
Typeset in Weiss

Printed in Canada
MAR

10 9 8 7 6 5 4 3 2

For Carole and Eric
May you be forever reunited on the other side

There are two things that interest me: the relation of people to each other,
and the relation of people to land.

—Aldo Leopold

CONTENTS

Preface

The Buddha once said, "Follow the truth of the way. Reflect upon it. Make it your own. Live it. It will always sustain you." Each day, we are given a unique chance to craft the type of life we want to live, from the friends we surround ourselves with and where we choose to live to the beliefs and attitudes we adopt.

I was first introduced to a form of Irish folk magick as a child and continued to learn about different traditions throughout my teenage years. Wicca was popular during that time, and the wheel of the year even more so. Growing up, I lived all over the United States: the tropics of South Florida, the Rockies of Montana, the high desert of Oregon, and so many other wonderful places. These areas had such different geographies and climates that each time we moved I found that what had once felt familiar became foreign and strange. I lived where it was hot when it should be cold; how does this fit in Yule?

These moves helped shape my idea of what it means to experience the wheel of the year. They made me think critically and ask questions such as, Can we still celebrate the wheel of the year as it is written if we don't live in a place where the climate matches the theme of the sabbat? What happens when the climate we live in is drastically different? How can we live in our own truth?

My truth is a direct reflection of my specific path of witchcraft. Folk witchcraft draws its knowledge from many places, mostly through word of mouth, passed down from generation to generation. I am an Irish American hereditary folk witch, but I haven't always been pagan. Throughout the years, I shed my Judeo-Christian religion and turned to a more left-hand path of paganism, crafting the unique practice I use today.

Each person, no matter where they live or what background they come from, has the ability to live intentionally each day. The combination of these days together forms the wheel of the year that we personally live by. Some may have a wheel of many holidays celebrating celestial events, secular holidays, and religious festivals. Others may compose their wheel of harvest seasons, lunar cycles, and climate conditions. That is what makes creating and celebrating your own unique wheel so fun.

Witchcraft is bold and unique, and there are no rules except the ones we set for ourselves. What is right on one person's path might not be right on our own. Celebrating the natural cycles and rhythm of the year is no different—and that is what this book is all about. There is no law that says all witches must celebrate Imbolc or Mabon. No one is going to come knocking on your door to let you know they think you're wrong for incorporating secular holidays such as Valentine's Day or Independence Day. Making space for freedom and pleasure in our daily lives will only ever impact us in positive ways.

When sitting down to write this book, I couldn't help but think back to my early years when I was still trying to grasp what it meant to be a witch. My mother was Irish Catholic and passed down to me a strong tradition of folk Catholicism. My father was a Buddhist convert whose convictions grew after the death of my mother. While I learned my folk traditions from my mother, my outlook came from my father—my concepts of life and death, suffering, and what it truly meant to be alive.

Through these two influential people I took away two of my most valuable life lessons: Never take information at face value and keep chasing my own inner truth. The year of the witch is not a year that belongs to me or any one witch, but to all witches collectively. It is a year when we as witches decide to live in our truth, taking back our power and our voice. What will you make of your year?

INTRODUCTION

Whether you've studied the wheel of the year in depth or just heard about it in passing, chances are high that you have had some form of run-in with this beloved pillar of modern witchcraft. Comprised of the eight sabbats of Samhain, Yule, Imbolc, Ostara, Beltane, Litha, Lughnasadh, and Mabon, the traditional wheel of the year is, on some level, part of most witches' daily and yearly practice. Not included in this version of the wheel are local seasonal celebrations, specific climate considerations, and your own unique traditions.

To some degree, we each practice our own year of the witch. This year can be comprised of birthdays and anniversaries, local and cultural holidays, religious and spiritual holidays, and vacation days. These years are fluid and change with us over time as we gain or lose family, start or end careers, move to a new place, and pursue our pathway of personal truth.

My goal with this book is to give you what you'll need to create your own personalized wheel of the year. In the following pages, we will explore the basic concepts of intuitively guided witchcraft, its role in the wheel of the year, the traditional wheel of the year, climate change, and more.

It's All in a Year

Today is the first day of the rest of the year. Tomorrow will also be the first day of the rest of the year. Looking at the year in this fashion means stepping outside of calendars and events and intentionally becoming present in the moment. This simple-sounding concept is deceptively difficult in practice and requires dedication and devotion.

Today, as people find their way to witchcraft, one of the first things they learn and copy into their journal or book of shadows is the wheel of the year. It is easy to know the dates and basic correspondences, but I have seen many struggle to harness and manifest the nuanced energy of each season as it passes by using just these sources.

In the past few years, I have taken an active role in teaching paganism and folk witchcraft online and in person, and I've noticed that when someone first starts on their path it is often the subtleties of the holidays that are overlooked in an effort to become "advanced" more quickly. To make matters worse, many sources would have you think that most modern religious holidays were directly and viciously stolen from pagans as the Catholic Church converted the folk religions of Europe. For these reasons, among many others, many novice witches discover they face challenges in developing an individual and intuitive wheel of the year practice. Through my own experience, I have found that a connecting with and practicing one's own intuitive wheel of the year starts at the most basic level—our day-to-day life.

The Year of the Witch

The year of the witch is the year of you. My biggest goal in writing this book has been to inspire a spark of change in witches both new and old to their path. By learning the origins, traditions, and alternatives to the wheel, it becomes easier to craft the reality we want on our own journey.

For the witch, every day of the year can become a sacred one. The year of the witch starts with you, and it starts right now. In the words of psychologist Charles Richards, "Don't be fooled by the calendar. There are only as many days in the year as you make use of. One man gets only a week's value out of a year while another man gets a full year's value out of a week."

Intuition, Intuition, Intuition

One of the most important skills the modern witch can develop is intuition. This skill is not easy to access, though, and there are many ways to lose touch with the intuitive sense. Throughout the pages of this book we will learn specific ways to practice intuitively guided witchcraft, how to grow more confident in your intuition, and how to use the wheel of the year to empower you in choosing your own methods to celebrate the changing of the seasons.

While intuition is widely talked about, I find that many beginners I teach will often ask what exactly it is and how it can be tapped into. Intuition can be broken down into three levels: passive intuition (complete guessing), intuition (moderate intuitional awareness), and educated intuition (active intuition). Intuitional awareness is especially relevant to this conversation of the wheel of the year and climate because a lot of what occurs outside can be felt through our body not only physically but also spiritually and intuitively.

Every sentient creature is capable of experiencing intuition, and most people experience some form of all three levels throughout the day. When we begin to focus and hone in on our practice of witchcraft, we expand our intuition from passive levels to mindfully active levels. Using active intuition is similar to how one would work a new muscle; the more you practice and develop it, the stronger and easier it is to use.

Higher Powers

Working with the wheel of the year fits into any secular, religious, or spiritual witchcraft practice. You don't have to observe any specific religion or creed to work with the rhythms of nature, and that is what makes it so special. When looking at the traditional wheel, the festivals mostly all observe some deity relating to Wicca. These gods and goddesses can be found in other forms of paganism as well and could even be recognized (while not worshipped) on a secular level.

For secular or more folky witches, the wheel of the year in its current form might seem scattered with religious overtones. So many times, I have come across beginners following a more secular path asking themselves how they can observe these festivals when they aren't working with those specific deities. By developing an intuitively based wheel of the year practice, secular witches are free to practice in a way that is genuine to their unique path.

On the journey to an intuitive year, everyone walks a different path. As such, everyone has preferred higher powers that they like to work with, whether that's the energy of the universe in a broader sense, or, more specific gods and deities. As we progress through this book, we will explore the world of land spirits and their role in daily and seasonal practice. Land spirits can be worshipped, called upon, and observed in any way a god or goddess may be, but they have the unique benefit of being tied directly to the land that we reside on. Working with land spirits and crafting a personal intuitive wheel are two pillars of developing a folk witchcraft path.

I

INTUITIVE WITCHCRAFT

*At times you have to leave the city of your comfort and go into the
wilderness of your intuition. What you'll discover will be wonderful.
What you'll discover is yourself.*

—Alan Alda

In my opinion, intuitive witchcraft is perhaps the best- and worst-kept secret of modern witchcraft. Why is intuitive witchcraft a best-kept secret if phrases containing "intuitive ___" are plastered across almost every social media outlet? In general, while the term is widely used, I have found that it is hard to uncover sources on expanding, deepening, and progressing intuitive witchcraft in an educated and informed manner.

Intuition is not a modern new age term, but is something much richer that has deeper psychological roots. In a 2008 article appearing in the *British Journal of Psychology*, "Intuition: A Fundamental Bridging Construct in the Behavioural Sciences," a group of researchers from Leeds University defined intuition as "the result of the way our brains store, process and retrieve information on a subconscious level." For most of us, the connection to and use of our intuition is natural enough to go unnoticed by our active conscious mind during our day-to-day lives. The way that we interact with our world today impacts our future intuitive responses. In this way, our intuition is constantly taking shape and changing, growing as we do both mentally and spiritually.

In terms of witchcraft, intuition is one of the most useful skills that we can develop. In spellwork, intuition can be tapped into to infuse spells with the magick of the witch. The witch can create spells that are unique to their path that can raise energy and power that is hard to find through other types of magick. As a note, I am in no way saying that prewritten or pre-worked spells aren't "good," because magick can be found anywhere we make it; however, harnessing the power of intuition in a controlled way can open a level of depth and understanding that we miss by relying fully on others' spellwork.

I have found that most witches call on and use their magickal intuition every day without even realizing it! Every time we recognize, feel, and read a person's energy without having interacted with them, we are calling on the power of our intuition. Some might say that this feeling is a form of psychic ability, but for the average person what they are experiencing is a heightened form of their intuition. In *Psychic Witch* Mat Auryn describes the difference of intuition and psychic ability, with intuition being "the unconscious processing of sensory information in one's environment to come to a particular conclusion" and psychic ability "the processing of extrasensory perception that doesn't rely on primary sensory information about one's environment." Auryn goes on to write, "intuition is based on perceivable external environmental information, whereas psychic ability is not."

Intuitive Spell Crafting?

In terms of spell crafting, it is often said that a beginner witch needs to learn to walk before they can run. In terms of complexity, intuitive spell crafting is deceptively easy to learn but takes practice to fully master. Many elements go into this type of spellwork such as season (time of year), celestial events, life changes, higher powers, intention, etc. It is important to explore not only what intuitive spell crafting is but also how you can use it to manifest the absolute most in your life and throughout the year!

Intuitive spell crafting is just what it sounds like: it's using intuition to guide and create rituals, spells, and manifestations within your life and the lives of those around you. The unique power of the witch is the ability to manifest with nothing more than their mind, magick, and the power of the universe. That might sound like some new age shtick, something that is simply too good to be true and would never work for the ordinary person, but it's not. This form of connected witchcraft requires a level of trust not only in yourself but in your practice and your understanding of magick.

There is a sacred quality to intuitive spell crafting, a mystery or sacrament in the relationship between witches and the cosmic energies of the universe. To empower your intuition as a guide along the winding road of your practice and personal craft is to make a pact with the elements of nature so that they can be called upon whenever you are working your own personal and unique style of magick.

There are energies where we live and work—spirits, flexible forces as changeable as the weather. When working with these energies, it is necessary to tune into their unique needs and temperaments while knowing that what works today might not work tomorrow.

Intuition Is a Muscle

At birth, the universe provides each of us with our own "gym," so to speak. This gym is not a physical place or even strictly speaking a spiritual place; it is a place where determination sows the seeds of future spiritual growth. That is to say, each of us is given all of the tools we will need to get in spiritual shape. This gift comes at no cost to us but requires dedication and determination. Some people will get further along in their training than others due to life circumstances and their degree of commitment. The human condition of jealousy and competition has no room here—individuals progress at their own pace regardless of how they decide to show it.

The most common questions asked by those beginning their path of witchcraft usually boil down to a variation on "Am I doing this right?" The question comes in all shapes and sizes: "Can I use this?" "When do I do that?" "What if . . . ?" The list goes on and on. These questions often indicate that someone is going too fast down the path of witchcraft, trying to run before they learn to walk.

Witches don't become skilled in their practice overnight, just as they don't become masters by reading one book. Spiritual skills are akin to a special muscle group; one cannot go to the gym, look at the equipment, walk away, and somehow get in shape without ever touching a single machine. Spiritual growth is the same. It requires time and effort.

To address some of these common questions when beginning to work with a witch's intuition, it is necessary to first learn how to distinguish between the voices of anxiety, ego, and intuition. When you are just starting out, it may be difficult to tell the difference. You have to learn how to truly hear these inner voices of your intuition. When I first started working in a 911 dispatch center, for example, I was amazed that everyone could tell the difference between a true emergency and a nonemergency call just by the tone of voice of the caller. Over time, I could also tell the difference without even trying. This level of unconscious understanding didn't happen overnight for me, and it might not for you, either.

Instinct versus Intuition

Instinct and intuition can seem similar, yet there are key differences, especially in the realm of conscious knowing and reason. Instinct is a biological reaction to outside stimuli that all animals are born with in order to keep them alive. Examples of instinct might be general fear of heights, dark places, and deep water. We are instinctually cautious in situations like this. Instinct looks and feels like an impulsive urge, a knee-jerk reaction to something occurring around us.

Intuition, on the other hand, is more complex. Intuition is the literal gaining of knowledge without any conscious thinking or reasoning. Intuition hardly ever comes in the form of an impulse. More often it feels like a lazy afternoon breeze flowing through our lives without any effort. The flow of intuition is always present, ready to be tapped into and explored.

Meeting Your Intuition

The best way to begin working with your intuition is to get in there, get your hands dirty, and get comfortable with it. This might feel awkward at first. Don't let this get in the way of taking the steps to an intuitively connected life. Meet your intuition halfway—it's there waiting for you whenever you're ready to take those preliminary steps into the wild unknown. When I feel a bit disconnected from my intuition, one of my favorite ways to reconnect is through a simple grounding ritual, like the one that follows. As you advance in your practice, you'll have your own grounding rituals for general maintenance of intuition.

GROUNDING RITUAL FOR AWAKENING
YOUR INTUITION

First, it's important that you get your mind and body ready—not just your spirit. Set aside some time to take a soothing bath, walk outdoors, prepare a nice meal, or do any other calming, solitary activity. Be intentional about the activity you choose! Once you feel as though you are in a physical, mental, and spiritual place of relative peace and calm, it is time to meet yourself and your intuition.

To begin, go to a place that is mostly quiet where you feel at peace. This might be a room in your house, a hill or mountain, a beach, or anywhere your feel comfortable and will not be disturbed.

Sit down with your back straight and your knees bent, feet planted on the ground in front of you. Close your eyes and take a deep breath in. As you exhale, let the clutter of your mind release with your breath. Repeat this a few times.

Once you have quieted your mind, think about a decision or situation you need to face soon. Visualize the event in your mind and listen to the voices that are speaking to you. What are they saying? Try to see if there are any differences in tone or quality of these thoughts.

Filter out the high-energy, high-pitched voices first. For example, if you are starting a new job soon, these thoughts might sound like, *I wonder how my new coworkers are. Am I going to be good at this job? What if I don't get along with my boss?* Breathe in, and breathe out all of the anxious and nervy thoughts. Those voices are not your intuition and are more closely related to your ego.

Notice the thoughts and voices that remain. This is when you can begin to see the difference between instinct and intuition. Remember that your intuition flows through you like a lazy river, peaceful in its knowledge that it is headed downstream and will get there when it gets there. There is no rush, no impulse to move faster or change course. This is the time to let the voices of your instinct go as well.

What you are left with is the solid conviction of your intuition. Listen to the voice and learn how it feels within you. Spend as much time as you can in this place, sitting with and acknowledging the profound wisdom that the universe shares with each of us. Your intuition is the guiding light of peace that will show you through stormy seas once you have learned to listen to it.

Practical Intuition

As you become more comfortable tapping into your intuition throughout the day and in all types of situations, listening to that voice will become second nature. However, even for the most practiced, every now and again we all have our doubts. The practical use of intuition is required of all witches, and there is no time more relevant for its use than in ritual and spellwork, selecting supplies, tools, and ingredients. So what exactly is practical intuition? I like to think of it as a compromise between the logical and the unseen. For example, when we pick out ingredients for a spell intuitively, practical intuition would have us realize that maybe we wouldn't put things like rose oil into a spell to sever ties with ex-lovers, like a cord cutting. In this way, we are using practical and logical reason in turn with our intuition to bring about the best set of results.

In my opinion, spellwork (especially intuitive science) is very much a science. Revisiting the theory that intuition is the result of the way our brains store, process, and retrieve information on a subconscious level, intuitive spellwork becomes something practical, measurable, and tangible. When you practice intuitive spellwork, you document what you will be doing and what you will be using, and then journal about the experience afterward. Come back to this entry a week and then a month later to analyze the spellwork, if it was successful and if there was anything that could have been changed. By documenting and revisiting your craft using this method, you are teaching your future intuition how to make better choices based on experience and mistakes. This process is not so dissimilar to the scientific method!

One of my earliest mistakes when I branched into spellwork was paying too much attention to doing things "the right way." This led to an overemphasis on things that frankly didn't matter and didn't help me progress. What I wish someone would have told me at the time was to not worry about what anyone else says or what is written on the internet. Instead, use the tools and words that are right for you. Just because something worked great for one person doesn't meant that something else couldn't equally work great for you. The more you pay attention to what your intuition has to say, the more the world will manifest for you before your eyes!

2

CYCLES, SEASONS, DEATH, AND REBIRTH

Birth is painful and delightful. Death is painful and delightful. Everything that ends is also the beginning of something else. Pain is not a punishment; pleasure is not a reward.

—Pema Chödrön

For most of us, our comfort is second nature; there is air-conditioning in the summer and heat in the winter. Fruits and vegetables of all kinds are sold year-round, whether they're in season or not. At heart, humans are creatures of comfort, always seeking out emotional and physical safety. We enjoy and thrive in the safety we create for ourselves indoors, insulated from the shifts in weather and subtle changes of the seasons. We become numb to the elements of the natural world. It is essential for witches to be able to flow with the energy of the earth and its natural cycles, but due to our modern-day lifestyle and the value we place on convenience, this can be surprisingly difficult. In essence, our comfort leaves us disconnected.

To grow is to feel uncomfortable as we expand beyond the confines of our current shell. Living in comfort is a balancing act and, unchecked, can become *counter*intuitive. The more comfortable we are, the less likely we will be to knowingly put ourselves outside of that comfort. In terms of modern living, this messes with our natural ability as humans to feel intimate with the changing energy of the seasons and to work with them (rather than against them) in our witchcraft. As witches, we connect to both the physical and spiritual world, restoring that relationship as humans with the natural cycles of the earth and its energy.

Human Cycles

One of the best life lessons that begins to put this theory in focus occurs in art class. When young students begin learning about perspective, two people looking at the same object from different angles will see two slightly different (or completely different) objects. This feeling is foreign, uncomfortable even. How can two people looking at the same object, in the same space, at the same time, have such different perceptions of what is happening? As a child, I'd always felt as though everyone in the room was in on some elaborate joke against me.

It is lessons like these that begin to shape our own personal cycles and the seasons of our lives. Other factors such as trauma, intimate relationships, pop culture, education, careers, and entertainment all play a major role in shaping the foundational seasons and cycles of how we move through our lives.

Most, if not all, things that we experience in the physical world are cyclical in nature: the way we act and react, how we make and break relationships, jobs and finances in general. As they say, when one door closes, another one opens. In the physical plane that we experience every day, we are oftentimes stuck in the same old rut looking for something to spice things up. The spiritual world is different, though. There, we can more easily choose to break a cycle or stay within bounds—we need only set our intention to effect a change.

Humans have two primary ways of creating their own cycles: in a solitary, singular way (cycles that directly affect one's daily life) and in a social way (political movements, economic booms and recessions, etc.). It's possible to use witchcraft to make local, national, or global change, and books such as *Revolutionary Witchcraft* by Sarah Lyons and *Witchcraft Activism* by David Salisbury are good sources for that social kind of work. However, because we are focused on personalizing our wheel of the year, tailoring it to suit our individual needs, we're going to focus in this book on solitary cycles.

Hormonal Cycles

Our solitary cycles are not only psychological but physiological and spiritual as well. One of the biggest factors acting on the human body in terms of health as well as mood is our hormone cycle. For example, through their magick women are able to tap into their fertility cycles, drawing power with the flow of energy during their moon time. My personal experience on and off birth control has taught me a lot about the natural cycle of feminine power and working with the flow of my natural cycles versus against them.

About a year ago, I was diagnosed with a migraine condition that required me to stop taking birth control. I watched as my body went into what I can only describe as pure shock. My body was so accustomed to taking a pill with hormones that it had seemingly forgotten its own natural cycle. My doctor assured me a million times over that this was not the case, that birth control doesn't permanently alter your rhythm. But personally, I'm not so sure. I reflected on why I was on the pill in the first place, and what it had done for me. I started taking birth control when I was sixteen, because I could. I was healthy, had no knowledge of my PCOS or migraine condition, and only wanted clearer skin. I was so willing to trade the power and sanctity of my period for the convenience of clear skin that for over a decade I took pills that stunted my natural magick.

It should go without saying, but men have natural hormonal cycles as well! Just because men don't bleed doesn't mean that this time of the month can't be used to tap into deeper levels of magick as well. Many medical researchers have agreed that the levels of testosterone and estrogen in men flow in cycles similar to women and can affect mood, sex drive, energy, appetite, and mental health.

Aside from hormones, we all experience physical cycles such as sleeping, eating, and other circadian rhythms. There is the popular old wives' tale that the body has all new cells every seven to ten years. This is technically false. Brain cells do not regenerate once they die and are never replaced. Most of our body, however, does replace and regenerate itself, so there is a cycle there too.

Seasons

Enjoying the changing of the seasons is one of the best parts of being alive and owning a body in this lifetime. The seasons of the earth dictate not only how we dress and celebrate but also what we eat, what we do for work and leisure, and where we go. There are more seasons than just autumn, winter, spring, and summer; there's also dry season, wet season, rainy season, Indian summer, shark season, and the list goes on. (That last one is really just for all of my Florida witches, but in certain locations there will be seasons for particular animals to be especially relevant.)

In autumn, we experience the beginning stages of decay in the living earth. The weather gets cooler and drier, the leaves begin to fall from the trees, and the veils between the world skip center. This is the time when death becomes present in our life. It may seem as though death is a far-off concept, something we don't understand, but through the seasons of autumn and winter we can begin to comprehend and familiarize ourselves with it. Death is a cycle that autumn welcomes with open arms.

Autumn is this period where it's equally hot but also slightly cooling down as we prepare to begin harvests. This is when the light begins to noticeably fade to dark faster, and we see the cycle of death rear its head again. We know that the energy of winter hasn't come in full force but are able to feel that it is right around the corner.

During the autumn months, the time to grow spiritually is in its most active stage. The veil between the worlds is thin, allowing spirits to walk with us. Gods make themselves known every day, and we see the cycles of life and death play out in nature. This time of year is especially useful for shadow work and resolving traumas. To take a quick pause here, I think it's important to recap what shadow work is and how it can play a role when working with seasons.

"Shadow work" is a phrase that was first used by the psychologist Carl Jung to describe the parts of ourselves that we repress from our active personality. Think of these as the skeletons in our psychological closet. On the topic of shadow work, Jung writes, "Unfortunately there can be no doubt that man is, on the whole, less good than he imagines himself or wants to be. Everyone carries a shadow, and the less it is embodied in the individual's conscious life, the blacker and denser it is. If an inferiority is conscious, one always has a chance to correct it. Furthermore, it is constantly in contact with other interests, so that it is continually subjected to modifications. But if it is repressed and isolated from consciousness, it never gets corrected."

When we talk about shadow work in a spiritual sense, we are going back to these fundamental ideas that Jung presented about examining ourselves wholly, shining light on parts that we would rather leave in darkness, and bringing balance to our overall psyche. Working on our shadow and doing shadow work is a lifelong process of keeping ourselves in check, feeling the pains and joys of our humanity, and working to be a better person as we make peace with our demons.

Looking at the wheel of the year, on a very surface level we see four major seasons: two are "light" and two are "dark." The energy of the earth quite literally guides us in working on and healing ourselves, giving us space annually to reevaluate and reinvent ourselves! Circling back to autumn and fall, which begins the dark half, aka the "shadow side" of the year, autumn is a good time to begin long-term money manifestation, being that it is the sister season to spring, which is useful for short-term or quick money manifestation (think the return of the sun and fire moving fast). Begin sowing the seeds of a long-term goal during autumn to see the sprouts and fruit of your labor in the spring and summer months!

As we move into winter, we fully embody living death and sleep. Sleep is often called the little death, and this is absolutely fitting for the season of winter. Earth is in a dormant state, and many of the gods have fallen asleep, seemingly leaving us to deal with the harsh realities of winter ourselves. These gods and goddesses will be reborn in the spring, but through the winter months it is bleak and cold without their presence to warm the skies.

Winter brings with it its own unique challenges, but it has many strengths that we can draw on. This is a time to develop personal drive and manifest a strong will into the next year. The divine feminine is in its fullest form in the winter months and is easiest to tap into during this time. The winter months are an incubation period between the death of winter and the life of spring, which is pregnant with possibility. The seeds waiting to take root in spring can only do so once they have gone through their dormant stage. Life needs rest, and winter presents the earth an opportunity for the healing sleep it needs in order to flourish in the spring.

Spring brings with it the first rays of new life, the joy and life-giving energy of the sun. It is a time of rebirth and return to harmony after the chaos of winter. Spring brings with it as much rain and sun as it does snow and ice, depending on the climate. It is a mixed time of year where the world of death meets the world of life—light and dark, yin and yang. The sun begins to stay out longer as we approach the summer solstice, and the earth begins to wake out of its dormant state.

Spring is bright and airy and brings with it the joy of potential. Magick is also reawakening from the long sleep of winter, and this is when we begin to see the seeds of many different types of manifestations. It is a time for love magick, and money magick, just as it is a time for fertility and friendship. The blossoms and new growth budding from the earth remind us to be thankful for the friendships and family relations that have survived to see the life of the new year.

Summer is the physical embodiment of life. It is a time when the sun is at its peak and the energies of fire, sexuality, and divine masculinity are at their strongest. All of the animals that were born through the spring months are growing, just as plants are growing. Storms are brewing in the Atlantic and the world is generally a warm and thriving place. Summer is the time to fulfill plans and manifestations that were started in the late winter and spring seasons.

Through these hottest months of the year, we find the fire and passion to continue manifesting our goals into reality. Tapping into this energy allows us to continue in our own personal cycles and live our best life before the pallor of autumn begins to set in. Summer is the time to follow through, and it is also the best time to perform baneful spellwork due to the high heat and generally insufferable humidity, storms, and high temperatures. Summer is also a great time to work on releasing our inner child and tapping into that creative energy. It is not a time to specifically work on our trauma, but to embody the fun and carefree energy of a child.

Climate Cycles

Through the years as I've begun to work more heavily with the energy of the wheel of the year, I have come to understand that climate cycles are perhaps the most influential cycle to that wheel. According to author

John Houghton, author of *Global Warming: The Complete Briefing*, climate is defined simply as the average weather in a particular region. Climate also describes annual variations of temperature, precipitation, wind, and other weather variables, per Francisco J. Borrero et al., in *Glencoe Earth Science: Geology, the Environment, and the Universe*. By this definition, climate is what determines seasons for particular regions, but that is not all it does. How humans have reacted to the changing seasons in their climates is a contributing factor to the formation of many of the holidays and celebrations that circle around the wheel of the year. In my opinion, this makes climate one of the most (if not the absolute most) important cycles to acknowledge.

I believe that climate variability has determined not only how humans evolved but also where and how quickly they evolved and developed technology for ease and survival. To this day we are still dealing with climate cycle issues much in the same way that can be felt through the echoes of history. Climate cycle issues are not limited to those involving human influence but also include natural variability, the carbon cycle, natural cycles such as El Niño, and many other factors. These cycles are something that will vary without human influence or interference but are affected in real, tangible ways by human practices.

When talking about climate, there are a few types of cycles that occur throughout years, decades, centuries, and millennia. On the shortest end of things, we have the annual decadal climate cycles that we see regularly. For example, El Niño or La Niña is a cycle that occurs every three to seven years and affects weather conditions throughout various parts of the world. El Niño is defined as a pattern of ocean surface temperature in the Pacific off the coast of South America, which has a significant influence on world climate (Houghton, *Global Warming*, 335). During El Niño, the

United States typically receives a flow of warm, dry air in the Northwest, which affects the fire cycle, while in the Southeast we receive heavy rainfall due to the change in wind shear and air currents.

Looking at a bigger picture of cycles, there are climate cycles that occur about every 200 to 1,500 years. These cycles are thought to be affected by ocean circulation patterns. There is historical evidence to back up these larger-scale patterns, which we know as the Medieval Warm Period and the Little Ice Age. The Little Ice Age occurred between AD 1400 and 1900. During this time frame, Europe was exceedingly colder than it had been during the Medieval Warm Period, which affected not only crops but human growth as well and was a driving factor in industrialization.

Lastly, the largest climate cycles occur every 10,000 to 100,000 years. These cycles are thought to be initiated by earth's change in orbit around the sun, which is known as the Milankovitch cycle. Christopher Campisano, an associate professor in the School of Human Evolution and Social Change at Arizona State University, says the Milankovitch cycle refers to Earth's natural orbital oscillation and includes three factors: eccentricity, obliquity, and precession (Campisano, "Milankovitch Cycles, Paleoclimatic Change, and Hominin Evolution"). In the cycle theory, there are three main components that combine to affect the amount of heat that is on earth's surface, which consequently influence our various climate patterns.

The first factor is earth's natural eccentricity, which refers to the elliptical path of its orbit around the sun. Second, we look at earth's axial tilt, also known as obliquity. Earth is constantly spinning around its own axis, which gives the planet day and night. This axis does not stay upright but tilts at angles between 22 and 24 degrees. Lastly, we have precession, which is essentially a gravity-induced wobble. A complete wobble cycle takes about 26,000 years and is caused by tidal forces created by the sun and moon.

There are a number of scientists who believe that due to the Milankovitch cycles, the global warming theory is actually a series of events that takes place every few thousand years and cannot be prevented. This argument posits that due to these factors of eccentricity, axial tilt, and procession, humans have little influence over the current cycle the earth is going through.

Astrological Cycles

I think it is fitting to put astrological cycles right after climate cycles for a number of reasons. First, in terms of basic earth science, both the moon and sun have daily physical effects on the earth that we can see with our own eyes. The sun warms the earth, pulling it along its path, while the moon shifts our tides. Astrological cycles are complex and abundant yet affect our day-to-day lives in many ways. Astrological cycles are known as synodic cycles, which are cycles that occur between one planet and other planetary interactions.

Each planet has its own specific cycle due to its orbit time and cycles around the earth. The moon has the quickest cycle, taking 27.5 days to travel through all twelve signs, whereas Pluto takes 248 years to travel through these same signs. The moon has additional observable cycles that influence the earth, such as when it goes through its phases, moving from the new moon and transitioning all the way through the full moon and back again.

The sun, Mercury, and Venus all travel the wheel in about 365 days. This means they move about 1 degree per day through the changing of the seasons. Mars takes a bit longer, about 22 months to travel through every sign. Jupiter takes about 12 years, Saturn approximately 28 years, Uranus 84 years, and Neptune 165 years. Pluto takes the longest, at 248 years.

In her book *Astrology for Real Life*, Theresa Reed groups these planets by their apparent cycle lengths. She writes,

> *There are three different groupings: personal planets, social planets, and the outer planets.*
>
> *The* **personal planets** *[the sun, the moon, Mercury, Venus, and Mars] move quickly through the sky and are thought to influence our personality as well as how we interact with other people. . . .*
>
> *The* **social planets** *[Jupiter and Saturn] symbolize the ways you operate in the world around you in addition to the social aspects of your life. . . . These . . . move through the cosmos at a slower pace, so their impact has a broader influence than the personal planets.*
>
> *The* **outer planets** *[Uranus, Neptune, and Pluto] . . . are the slow-moving heavyweights in the cosmos. They represent what's happening in the world or society.*

Looking at the orbit lengths and pairing them with the planet groupings, we can make a real connection between the cycles, elements (more on this later), and the energy throughout the wheel of the year.

The Astrological Signs of the Year

In terms of astrology, it is common knowledge that there are twelve signs that cycle through the year:

Aries	March 21–April 19
Taurus	April 20–May 20
Gemini	May 21–June 20
Cancer	June 21–July 22
Leo	July 23–August 22
Virgo	August 23–September 22
Libra	September 23–October 22
Scorpio	October 23–November 21
Sagittarius	November 22–December 21
Capricorn	December 22–January 19
Aquarius	January 20–February 18
Pisces	February 19–March 20

Additionally, each astrological season has a planet (or planets) that rules over it and lends it unique flavor!

Sun	Leo
Moon	Cancer
Mercury	Gemini, Virgo
Venus	Taurus, Libra
Mars	Aries
Jupiter	Sagittarius
Saturn	Capricorn
Uranus	Aquarius
Neptune	Pisces
Pluto	Scorpio

Laid out like this, it is easier to see the link between the synodic cycles and day-to-day astrology!

These orbits are the general cycles of the planets and their respective signs, but they are not the only types of patterns that impact the earth astrologically. Other key cycles include patterns such as retrogrades. A retrograde happens when earth passes or is being passed by another planet. This makes a backward movement illusion, as the planets are revolving around the sun in the same direction but at different speeds. Every planet maintains its own retrograde cycle. The quickest retrograde cycle is Mercury, which only lasts about 21 days. The longest retrograde cycle is Neptune, which lasts about 158 days.

When All Good Things Come to an End

German philosopher Arthur Schopenhauer reminds us, "Each day is a little life: every waking and rising a little birth, every fresh morning a little youth, every going to rest and sleep a little death." Death is the one cycle that begins and ends it all. Death is a constant companion to the cycles of our life in nature and walks silently with us through all the joys of life.

The cycle of death begins before birth, as we navigate through death to the light of new life. Depending on what you believe happens before and after life, that is going to shape your opinion on the beginning cycle of death. There is no witch canon: some witches are atheistic and believe nothing happens, while others believe in reincarnation, and still others believe in heaven- and hell-type places. I personally believe in reincarnation, so out of death comes life. Death is a dormant state and can be observed in seeds that have no measurable life as you plant them in the ground, yet become beautiful plants and flowers after some time. Out of the darkness of death comes the light of life.

Acknowledging and coming to peace with the cycles of life and death are important for the modern witch's spiritual path. We can't avoid death, and it is not as scary as it is made out to be through our limited understanding. Humans are often fearful of what we do not know, and death is something we do not know. We do not remember it after we're born; the light of day erases the knowledge of darkness that our souls knew before. However, we all did come from death, and we all will return to it.

3

ELEMENTAL MAGICK

Move swift as the Wind and closely-formed as the Wood.
Attack like the Fire and be still as the Mountain.

—Sun Tzu, The Art of War

What is elemental magick, and why is it relevant to intuitive witchcraft? In a nutshell, elemental magick works with and calls on the elements to manifest specific outcomes and goals. There's not a single person who goes through their day without experiencing any of the elements. We may walk outside in the morning and feel a breeze, go for a walk and sense the heat of the sun on our skin. We could water our plants, or choose to compost/recycle. All of these experiences are simple ways that we experience (and sometimes take for granted) the elements, often without much pause.

On the most basic level, we have four elements: fire, earth, water, and air. But those of us who are pagans know there is a fifth element: spirit. The average person can't interact with, see, or physically feel spirit, but that doesn't mean it isn't there. I don't personally work with this element, but just because I don't do something doesn't mean it isn't something to examine and be aware of.

I would be remiss to touch on elements without briefly hitting alchemy. In *The Dark Arts*, Richard Cavendish writes, "In modern occultism the four elements are four conditions in which energy can exist. Fire stand[s] for electricity, air is the gaseous state, water the liquid state and earth the solid state. All things exist in one or other of these conditions, or in a mixture of them, and one condition can be changed into another."

In our day-to-day lives, we perceive most things to relate to one primary element (think plants as earth), but nothing on the physical plane is made up of one single element alone. Without water and earth, we wouldn't have plants; without earth and fire, we wouldn't have crystals and gems; without air, we wouldn't have fire. The elements lend each other their strengths, and in doing so lend us the energy of their strengths as well. Let's take a look at each of the five elements in a little more depth.

Fire

Fire is a strong element of life, love, and passion. It is associated most often with the sun and governs aspects such as desire, intuition, intellect, and manifestation. On the flip side, fire can be as destructive as it is creative. It is an element that requires patience and care, because if it gets out of control it has the potential to destroy everything around it. Governing the south aspect of the compass of life, the fire element relates closely to our outward personalities (think sun sign in astrology).

Fire can be invoked in many different ways. The more obvious way is with a literal flame. This flame can be in the form of a candle, match, bonfire, or even electronic candle. Additionally, there are ways to invoke this element that don't require any purchases or tools. The sun is a great way to invoke fire. Additionally, the passion of sex can be used to invoke each of the elements separately, but especially the fire and earth elements.

Earth

Earth is the strongest element of stability. The earth is a versatile element, having strengths in both growth and death, present through all the various cycles of life. Unlike fire, the earth has an abundance of features such as forests, deserts, mountains, beaches, and plains that can play into and diversify this element magickly.

One of the unique factors about the earth element is that it can exist independent of other elements, and it can also coexist uniquely with each of the other elements. Water, fire, and air each have unique ways that can literally change and alter the physical condition and makeup of the earth element, leading to magickly tied energy and elements. When working with the earth, it is important to remember that it can be as destructive as it is stable. Earthquakes and volcano eruptions are examples of how stability can be altered drastically with the addition of other elements, pressure, and stress over long periods of time.

The earth element is associated with the cardinal direction north. While not a traditional correspondence, I like to associate the moon with the earth element. The moon is an extension of life on earth, lending to the ebbs and flows of our tides and cycles. It is guided by the gravitational pull of the earth and in return gives us the movement through the other elements that provide life through our planet.

Invoking the earth element is as simple as walking outdoors and making the conscious decision to be a part of the earth. Walking outdoors, whether it is in the rain, heat, snow, sun, or night, is a great way to experience the energy of the earth. Other ways to connect include gardening, composting, working with animals, and cooking. There is hardly anything more grounding than taking the time to walk up to a tree, putting your hand against it, closing your eyes, and taking a deep breath. By doing this simple practice, witches are able to connect with the grounding energy of the earth and feel literal mountains being lifted off their bodies and spirits.

Earth can also be invoked through kitchen magick. Cooking with vegetables, fruits, and roots brings the earth element into our kitchens and into our physical bodies, imbuing us with nutrients and life-giving energy. If you live in an urban area or an apartment, kitchen witchcraft is one of the easiest ways to welcome in and invoke the earth element.

Water

Don't let water pass you by—it is stronger than you think. Water is the element of the source that sustains all life. No plant or animal could survive without it, which makes it the most important element that there is (water witches everywhere, rejoice!). What makes water unique and especially versatile is that it can exist as a solid, liquid, or gas. It can come as a river, fog, steam, or ice. It can come to us as snow, hail, sleet, or rain. Water not only purifies us but also heals us, sustaining our life force more than any other element.

Water, just like every other element, has the power to destroy. Unlike fires or earthquakes, though, water floods us in ways that the other elements simply cannot. When combined with air, water can create hurricanes and storms of massive proportions. One only has to think back to Hurricane Katrina or Superstorm Sandy to be reminded of the damage that water can inflict.

While it is said that water is most closely related with the moon (due to the moon's effect on the tides), I believe that water is most closely related to Neptune. Neptune is considered both an ice and gas giant, made up of fluid "icy" materials including water. Neptune rules Pisces, and it is associated with intuition and spiritual enlightenment. The element of water is associated with west on the compass of life.

There are many ways to invoke the element of water in your everyday life. One of the easiest ways is to drink water intentionally, welcoming in the healing properties of this element. We all shower, swim, and brush our teeth with water. We cook with water, and we give our plants and animals life-sustaining water. We can also intentionally invoke the element of water through connecting with natural bodies of water!

Going to places like the beach, lakes, or rivers are ways that can ground us to the elements of water and earth. If you happen to live somewhere where finding all of these elements is a little bit hard, you can always fall back on man-made swimming pools or water fountains.

Air

Air is versatile and an element of movement, similar to water. The element of air is always present around us on earth, but usually isn't noticeable until we lack it or feel inconvenienced by it. For those who live in colder climates, air can be physically seen as they talk outside during the winter. It's not uncommon to become out of breath while hiking in the mountains. In times like this, it is common for people to express sentiments about the "air being thin."

I like to think that air is unique in its transformative life-giving (and life-taking) powers. For example, a fire without air is extinguished. Air is vital for life to thrive, especially on earth. It is a sacred resource, something that we take into our bodies instinctually to sustain us. A person could live without water or food for a few days, but it only takes a few minutes without air to extinguish the life it once sustained. As such, air is most associated with east and gods in general. Additionally, any of the gas giant planets can be associated with the air element.

The easiest way to invoke the element of air is through meditation. When we meditate, we focus on our breathing, which means we are literally taking in and letting out air within our physical bodies and spirit. Other ways to experience the air element include walking outdoors during a particularly windy day, turning on the air-conditioning if you live in a warm place, or even going outdoors during a particularly hot and sticky day. That might seem counterintuitive, to intentionally make yourself uncomfortable, but experiencing the earth and elements without the breeze helps to highlight how important it actually is!

Spirit

Last but certainly not least is the element of spirit. Spirit inhabits every essence of our being. We learn how to relate to the world through our spirit, and once we are done with the world in this form, we return to spirit. Spirit cannot be contained or quantified in any specific sort of way. That does not mean it is not there; it just means that we are not aware of it.

Spirit encompasses the divine feminine, the divine masculine, and the divine other energies. This is to say, it is truly a gender-neutral element. Spirit is at once everything and nothing, being a part of all that has ever been, all that will ever be, and all that will never come to pass. To invoke spirit is to invoke the essence of being, and the essence of being cannot be contained.

The spirit element is symbolized in the topmost point on a pentacle or bottommost point on a pentagram and is said to symbolize us, ourselves. There is a lot of conflicting information out there about the difference between the pentagram, ☆ or ⛧, and the pentacle, ⊕.This tends to be because each tradition uses them slightly differently. Some people use either word to mean the same symbol regardless of whether its upright or inverted, while some use the word *pentacle* to refer to an upright five-pointed star surrounded by a circle and *pentagram* to refer to an inverted five-point star.

In *The Essential Golden Dawn*, Chic and Sandra Cicero define pentacles as "one of the four tarot suits attributed to the element of earth and the Qabalistic world of Assiah. A pentacle is a magical diagram, usually round, inscribed on parchment, metal, or some other material to create a talisman. Also, one of the elemental tools of a Golden Dawn magician."

They go on to define pentagram as "A geometric figure based on the pentangle, which has five lines and five 'points.' Figures based on the pentangle include the pentagram and the pentagon. The pentagram or five-pointed star is attributed to the five elements of fire, water, air, earth, and Spirit. Sometimes called the 'Blazing Star,' 'wizard's foot,' the 'Star of the Magi,' and the 'Star of the Microcosm.' Also called the pentalpha because it can be constructed out of five Greek alphas."

Spirit is present in every element, strengthening everything it touches. It is unquantifiable and arousing in its mystery. Spirit as an element is invoked through everything that we do. Intentional living, intuition, spiritual practice, meditation, and prayer are the most common ways to invoke spirit. Spirit is not invoked only by pagan practitioners or new age spiritualists, but by every religion and spiritual practice on this planet.

Spirit comes to us on the level that we are able to understand. How one person sees and understands spirit will inherently be different than how someone else does. God meets us on our own level, which means that spirit meets us there as well. We understand and grow at our own pace, with our spirit as our guide. Take time to sit alone and meditate. You'll find that you're sitting with your spirit and are able to listen to the wisdom it holds.

Calling Down the Elements

Each of the four base seasons has a primary element that can be specifically drawn on to aid spellwork. When calling on the elements, we can use the power of the seasons to evoke particular energy! I think connecting seasons with elements is a really cool concept, and it has allowed me to gain a deeper relationship with the natural world and its elements seasonally. Thinking back to the pentagram and the elements of fire, water, earth, air, and spirit, we can begin to match seasons with their respective elements.

Spring embodies the element of air. It is fresh with new life, and stepping outside you can feel the breeze against your skin in ways that would be uncomfortable in almost any other season. Throughout time, people have literally described spring as "light and airy." When calling down the element of air and spring, use white, sky blue, light pink, and light yellow candles.

Summer is full of fiery heat and embodies the element of fire. The sun is hot and heats the earth. If you were to spend enough time in the sun during summer, you might even receive a physical burn. Use red, orange, bold yellow, brown, white, and gold candles to call down the element of fire and summer.

Fall is my favorite season and brings with it feelings of comfort, stability, and peace. Fall embodies the element of the earth. It is the end of the witch's year, a time to ground, wind down, and reflect on the year. Use green, purple, brown, gray, black, yellow, and burnt orange candles when calling down the element of earth and fall.

Winter is both the death of the past year and the beginning of the new one. Winter embodies the element of water to many places that receive snow. In climates where it is warmer, water becomes a source of joy, as the sun is away and water nourishes gardens and beaches. When calling down the element of water and winter, use silver, gray, white, blue, light blue, purple, red, black, or green candles.

Lastly, there is the element of spirit. I believe that spirit fits into every season, filling the gaps between the transitions and providing a steady presence and foundation for each time to have its moment. Spirit is ever present and can be called upon anytime one needs a boost of strength. I personally like to use white candles to call down spirit in the spring and summer, and black candles in the fall and winter. I do this because it reflects the human–spirit journey through the dark and light halves of the year and reminds us where our minds should be working.

4

SHEPHERDING THE LAND

The world is not given by his fathers, but borrowed from his children.

—Wendell Berry, *The Unforeseen Wilderness*

Initially, this chapter was written before the onset of what we now know as SARS-CoV-2, aka COVID-19. I think it is important to point that out because due to this new element, the way in which the world functions and my opinions on it have altered significantly. In the face of global panic, the true state of the world and its downfalls were made crystal clear. As I write this now, it is spring of 2020, and the world is at a standstill. Nothing like this has been seen in modern history (where literally the whole globe shut down), and I'm not sure we will ever see something like this again. It is too early to say what will be the outcome of all of the changes, positive or negative, but without a doubt things will never be the same.

Throughout the course of humanity, people have largely held the role as shepherd/steward to the earth and its bounty. Our ancestors did not view this role through rose-tinted glasses and knew that their lives and the lives of their ancestors were often difficult and grueling. Living off of and with the land in a more rural setting can be physically taxing, cold, and bleak. This was a life that was often fraught with poverty, hunger, and disease. When we think back to what we consider simpler times, we view things through the privilege of survival. These were harsh times, with Mother Nature being a hard and inconsistent mistress.

While today we often have what we need to survive, our ancestors were not always so lucky due to long winters, plague, frost, draught, and famine. Fast-forward to the plights of the modern human and witch. Most of us live in a materialistic society filled with pavement and the pleasures of urban and suburban areas. We are out of balance with not only ourselves but the very earth, its cycles, and its seasons. This fact has become strikingly apparent with the rise of a modern pandemic. When faced with a crisis, many of us do not know how to conduct ourselves because we are simply unable to source our own food and water outside of a marketplace.

In some of my more reclusive phases, I have thought a lot about how I believe humans, myself included, have lost touch with the cycles of birth, life, and death, focusing instead on temporary comfort. When I was nineteen, I overheard one of the most profound things that changed the way I relate to the world and my life. I was pregnant at the time, and my emotions were running pretty high, which is why this probably stuck out to me the way it did. I had gone to Publix, which is a local supermarket, and got in line to check out. A man in front of me was chatting with the cashier. It became apparent very quickly that he was not from the area due to his accent. The cashier noticed this as well and asked the man what brought him into the city. He said, "I wanted to have an adventure, but I miss home. It seems as though I've traded a life of meaning for a life of convenience."

This truth, spoken so frankly by a stranger, struck me to my core. After leaving the store, I went back and wrote this thought into my journal to reflect on. I have thought about it nearly every day since, years later, the tone and weight of this idea pushing me out of my comfort zone. To me, it was impactful that a stranger chose to be raw and honest in a culture of politely disconnected hellos and thank-yous. Because of this honesty, my eyes were violently and quickly opened to my own role in what he described as "convenience." If I were being honest with myself, I would have said I wasn't connected, in tune, or aware of the earth around me because I didn't see it.

What is amazing is that more and more people have begun to wake up to this as well due to COVID-19. In a recent *Atlantic* article,

Marina Koren talks about four distinct ways that the quarantine and stay-at-home orders have affected the earth. The first marked way is there is less rumbling on the surface of the earth, due to the drop in use of public and private transportation. Second, there is less air pollution due to fewer people traveling and more factories being closed. Third, city soundscapes are changing. Lastly, ocean noise pollution is down.

I believe that the third point, changing city soundscapes, is the most impactful point in the whole piece because it highlights just how out of touch urban dwellers have become with the natural world. Koren writes,

> City dwellers might now be hearing sounds that can get muffled by the usual drone. Rebecca Franks, an American who lives in Wuhan, the epicenter of the coronavirus outbreak in China, made this observation 48 days into the city's quarantine last month: "I used to think there weren't really birds in Wuhan, because you rarely saw them and never heard them. I now know they were just muted and crowded out by the traffic and people," Franks wrote on Facebook. "All day long now I hear birds singing. It stops me in my tracks to hear the sound of their wings." Sylvia Poggioli, an NPR correspondent in Italy, reported that the streets of Rome are so empty, "you can actually hear the squeak of rusty door hinges," and "the chirping of birds, an early sign of spring, is almost too loud."

I love that last quote especially: "the chirping of birds, an early sign of spring, is almost too loud." What'an impactful thought when put against the reality that many people have lost touch with the natural world. In a city that is usually alive with deafening sound, the natural noises of nature can seem to be too much. I think this really puts into perspective how, even as we find ourselves more and more connected, we may not be connected to the things that truly matter. Collectively, we have lost sight of what it means to be a shepherd of the land and why being a shepherd is important.

What Is a Shepherd?

Simply put, a shepherd is someone who watches over the welfare and safety of the lives that have been entrusted to them. Our earth is not so different from a living animal, in that we are responsible for taking care of it and maintaining its health and well-being. As witches, it is especially important to be the shepherds and protectors of the lands we reside upon. These lands are not just dirt and soil, but living entities with spirits and energies that affect us in ways we do not fully understand.

In urban America, there is a culture where the norm is to do more for less, cut corners, adopt a "me me me" attitude, and pack schedules to the point of exhaustion. Quick consumption has replaced intentional action. How many people use disposable silverware or plates to avoid doing dishes? How many people use disposable, single-serve coffee pods instead of reusable filters? How many acres of forests, prairieland, and wetlands have been lost to build a parking lot or building? I am reminded of the words Joni Mitchell and, later, Counting Crows, sang about paradise and parking lots.

Urban humanity has lost sight of the spirit of the land, especially in capitalistic societies where it's more convenient and comfortable to be connected and plugged in than anything else. While I am not Christian, I grew up in an area where public schools are poorly managed and parents send their children to private schools whenever possible. Being a pagan witch in a Christian school was a task unto itself, but some of the most memorable lessons I learned were about the concept of land ownership in the Old Testament:

> *The land must not be sold permanently, because the land is mine*
> *[God's] and you reside in my land as foreigners and strangers.*
> *(Leviticus 25:23)*

We are living as though we own the world, when in reality we are guests here, passing through for a very short time. No one truly owns the land, yet we have accepted the division and monetization by a select few who "control" these spaces and pay extraordinary amounts of money for what the earth has provided freely. Our job is to be a shepherd to our planet, our only planet, and take care of it.

Quick consumerism (think fast fashion and factory farming) is the antithesis of shepherding the land. It is not sustainable or conscious of the people, tools, and materials that it uses. To be truly connected to the land, it is important to be conscious of the social factors that impact the direct health and energy of the spirits around us. This is not to say that buying into modern methods of production is inherently evil in nature, but if someone has the ability to make a more sustainable and impactful choice, it is their duty to do that to shepherd the land. Easy additional ways to live a more natural and unburdened lifestyle include going to the farmers market instead of a mass supermarket chain or buying secondhand clothing instead of fast fashion.

Sustainability is definitely a marketing buzzword these days, and brands can be deliberately misleading about what is sustainable and what is not. When in doubt, maintaining intentional practices such as reducing consumption overall, reusing what you already have instead of buying new things, recycling items you no longer need, and buying sustainable, green products from trusted companies are some basic ways that people shepherd the land. Thinking about the scale of pollution can be overwhelming, but what matters most is making your shepherding an intentional choice.

There will come a time when your view of how we treat the earth will be irrevocably changed. It may be something you see in a movie, a natural or man-made disaster, or simply spotting trash washing up on your favorite beach. Whatever it is, use that passion to fuel the ritual below. Its purpose is to turn over our conveniences for in-depth meaning, to change ourselves from users to protectors.

BECOMING A SHEPHERD

Before we begin, it is important to stop and take a solid look at yourself and what you can improve on. Sit down with a blank piece of paper, and draw a line down the middle to create two columns. On the left-hand side, write down the things you need to work on to be more sustainable and intentional. On the right-hand side, write down what you could do to change these things.

Here are some examples:

Things I can improve	WAYS TO IMPROVE
Using single-use water bottles and plastic products	Purchasing and using a metal or glass water bottle and other reusable products
Buying out-of-season produce that's shipped in from thousands of miles away	Buying food from the farmers markets and local co-op
Generally overconsuming	Buying in bulk and recycling as much as possible

Once you've finished your list, fold the paper three times. Next, for each item that you listed, purchase a seed or seedling that can survive outside with minimal to no help (native plants).

When you have assembled your seeds, go to an area on your property that you feel connected to or that has been generally neglected. Sitting on the ground, arrange everything in front of you: your list, your seeds, and maybe a trowel for planting.

Place your hands directly in the soil and close your eyes, feeling the energy of the earth joining the energy of your body through your hands. Visualize a golden light coming through your body into the earth, and a silver light coming from the earth into your body from every point of contact. As this silver light enters you, feel the change and charge of the soil breathing into your spirit.

When you are ready, open your eyes and pick up your list. In your own words, ask the spirits of the land to listen and be present with you. Speak your covenant to the earth, reading aloud each way that you have fallen and each way that you will make a change. In this way, you are joining the earth in a journey of love and acceptance, protection and healing.

Once you have read your list, it is time to plant your seeds. These seeds will be the physical embodiment of your covenant between yourself and the earth. It is important to plant them with care and tend to them each day. You are now the literal shepherd of these lives, and it will be your responsibility to care for them to the best of your ability.

This ritual can be repeated, modified, and reaffirmed multiple times a year. I typically do all of my seasonal planting with this ritual and do my harvests with a separate one. The earth will take care of us if we take care of her, and by taking care of these plants we are able see and feel with our physical bodies the relationship between ourselves and Mother Earth.

Smoke Cleansing

Smoke cleansing is the practice of burning herbs, incense, woods, resins, and other items for the purpose of clearing a space or preparing for spellwork. It is believed that the smoke cleans, invokes, and manifests, and it's a practice that has been a feature of most cultures and religions worldwide. There are so many materials that can be used for this purpose, depending on your culture, climate, and accessibility.

In the new age community, the term *smudging* has become increasingly popular over the past few years. "Smudging," "white sage," and "how to smudge" have been popular search terms for the past ten years, showing a large uptick in searches and popularity (from *trends.google.com*) since 2010. While *smudging* has become synonymous with *smoke cleansing*, it is not the same thing.

The word *smudge* is English and derived from a fifteenth-century word, *smogen*, meaning to soil, stain, or blacken. In modern context, however, the word shifted to refer to the Native American smoke cleansing practice. Modern smudging typically refers to the Native American spiritual practice that uses *Salvia apiana*, *Salvia officinalis*, tobacco, sweetgrass, yarrow, and juniper for cleansing, purification, and healing rituals. These rituals were/are conducted by a trained shaman or healer who sources their herbs using traditional methods.

The issue that many find with the use of the term *smudging*, and what makes it appropriative, is that people engaging in this now mainstream and commercialized practice have lost a connection with what makes it sacred while simultaneously only observing the parts of the practice that suit them (for example, lighting sage to clear negative energy without any additional effort or spiritual input). While there are arguments that *smudging* isn't appropriative because it's an English word, I disagree. I've listened to the voices of indigenous people and reflected on what their narrative means to me, spiritually and in practice. I don't think the majority of people practicing this have done the same.

So if not smudging, then what? Every culture throughout history has used smoke to heal and cleanse. Churches use incense, the Scottish have a practice called *saining*, in India incense has been used hand in hand with their spirituality and religion for longer than the word *smudge* has even existed. There is a space for any and all of us to use smoke to cleanse and heal our bodies. I think the best supplies we can have when using smoke to cleanse and heal come from things we grow and source ourselves. I suggest growing your own sage, rosemary, lemongrass, cedar, eucalyptus, and even bay leaves. All of these plants can be grown conventionally and sustainably at home (and on a patio) and are great for cleansing. Additionally, incorporating local hand-harvested flowers and botanicals adds an extra kick of conscious land magick.

Other plants you might incorporate into your smoke cleansing rituals include mugwort, lavender, mint, pine, juniper, catnip, dandelion, fern, heather, or peat. It should be noted that different plants have different properties and purposes, and it is really up to each individual witch to try them all and decide what is best for you and your practice!

Here are a few of my favorite plants:

Myrrh—for supporting mental health and purifying spaces

Lemongrass—for road opening and communication with ancestors

Juniper—for protection and abundance

Mint—for supporting lung health and to bring clarity

Rosemary—for easing grief and cord cuttings

A BASIC SMOKE CLEANSING RITUAL

After going through the motions of day-to-day life, we sometimes find we are running a little ragged. We might clean our physical spaces, take a bath, go for a jog. In these moments, I find that doing a basic smoke cleanse of my physical body works wonders in lifting my spirits. It's pretty basic to do and will have you feeling brand-new in no time!

You will need:

- A small white candle (a chime or tealight works best)
- A dried herb bundle, loose herbs and charcoal, or incense
- Lighter or matches

In a bathroom or other uncarpeted area, begin by lighting your white candle. Sit on the floor cross-legged or in a chair if you are unable to sit on the ground comfortably. Close your eyes and focus on your breathing. Tuning into your body, feel where any tension or held emotions might be stored.

Imagine a warm light traveling across your body, starting in your toes and moving up through your legs into your body, arms, and head. Allow this light to linger and loosen up these tense areas.

When you are ready, light your incense and stand up. Starting from your feet, circle your body with the smoke in a clockwise motion. Allow yourself to breathe in the smoke, and as you exhale, allow the smoke to travel out, releasing any stored tension, energy, or emotion.

When you have circled your whole body, allow the incense or herbs to finish burning with the candle.

5

AT THE GATES OF WITCHCRAFT

It's easy to fictionalize an issue when you're not aware of the many ways in which you are privileged by it.

—Kate Bornstein

This section gets a bit personal to me, and to many I feel like would fall into the category of lower- or working-class witch. During my time creating content in the public eye, the term *plastic witchcraft* has been thrown at me on public forums, direct messages, and emails typically after I give tips for budget witchcraft. I see myself and others routinely get called a "plastic witch," and am told that I promote "plastic witchcraft," which was harmful not only to "real witches" but to the environment as well. The people who fling this term around are often not working-class, and speak from a place of spiritually bypassing privilege.

I believe the term *plastic witchcraft* is twofold in its meaning. First, "being plastic" refers to being superficial and fake, like the Plastics clique in the movie *Mean Girls*. Second, being deemed a plastic witch literally refers to using plastic products. However, the term itself is very condescending and shows an aggressive amount of spiritual bypassing. That is to say, calling someone a "plastic witch" often takes empathy out of the equation and allows for more privileged witches to ridicule and scorn less fortunate witches.

Another factor that compounds the issue is that there are people who enjoy the aesthetic of witchcraft. There is nothing wrong with embracing the things that bring you joy, but it makes the divides between different camps in witchcraft fairly obvious. There are those who don't care at all about aesthetics and just practice, regardless of anyone's opinion. There are those, like me and many others, who have a strong online presence but don't really adhere to any specific aesthetic. And then there's the last category, who have a strong online presence or strong personal presence with a carefully crafted aesthetic, usually found on YouTube and Instagram.

Having an aesthetic does not mean that your witchcraft is any less genuine or real. I do not consider myself to be a plastic witch, but I understand that some people might think that because I have a strong online presence, I am somehow less genuine. I'll just say this: at the end of the day, only *you* are going to be able to know if your practice is true or "plastic."

Western society has capitalized on the aesthetic of witchcraft. After years of being hidden, we have become a target market that is surprisingly willing to drop a lot of money on our spiritual practices. You can buy cheap witchcraft supplies online from China, or at the dollar store, or in Whole Foods even! This ease of access creates a disconnect between what is spiritually bound and what is impulse bound for our spiritual purchases.

Our energy creates the money we have to spend, so as we spend our energy, it is important to be intentional about who and what we support when we spend it. Amazon has become a staple for many witches due to ease of access and ability to search and read reviews. What this process takes away is the chance to learn firsthand from other witches and support local communities and keep those resources in place. Shopping small is a step any witch can take on a grassroots level to build up and support the things that matter to them!

A quick glance through Instagram or Tumblr will bring tons of pictures of aesthetically pleasing, new agey, lightworking witchcraft photos. As scrolling becomes a way to disconnect from our physical worlds, we are thrust into the virtual world of aesthetically targeted and marketed witchcraft. It doesn't take much effort to find altars full of figures and candles and crystals, or conversely shelves and shelves of books, and you'll want to have them. It becomes something that we can compare ourselves to, something that marks us as "devoted."

This aesthetic version of witchcraft is like witchcraft on steroids. Personally, I've never felt as though I connect to hoarding tons of statues, or crystals, or herbs. I do collect books, but I also read all of my books and find they are useful to my personal growth. Enjoying something and wanting lots of it doesn't make you any less of a witch, just as not having lots of things doesn't make you any less of a witch. Witchcraft is, at its heart, your strength and ability to manifest your desire with what you have right in this very moment.

We are being sold products that pander to the new age and lightworker communities rather than witchcraft directly. A good friend of mine, Dr. Timothy Heron, has pointed out both in personal conversations with me and in his talks that witches are not the same as lightworkers. I do tend to agree with his opinion, but I do not intend to gatekeep witchcraft from anyone that uses either term. Instead, I'd like to show the clear and obvious divide in terminology. I believe his words sum up a good distinction between the two without much bias:

> There is confusion between pagan beliefs and new age beliefs. . . .
> Witchcraft is a practice that is usually rooted in pagan thoughts. . . .
> New age practice [includes] the following: a deep attraction to crystals, energy healing, and to transcending their bodies rather than being grounded. The focus is much more spiritual than earth centered.

The way that witches, and pagans in particular, become a part of the natural world around us is part of what makes us different! Witches aren't a group of consumers to be sold to; they are part of an ancient connection to the energy of the earth regardless of aesthetic or superficial approval.

Witchcraft Is Inherently Anti-consumerism

Another issue that the internet seems to have with plastic witches is accessibility. I like to put accessibility with gatekeeping and privilege, because it really does keep some of the more disenfranchised population in the witchcraft community at the "gate," so to speak. With books on witchcraft being written similarly to cookbooks, beginners just starting out might feel as though they need a ton of supplies to be "real." First and foremost, this narrative is wrong, and it leaves many beginners unsure of how and where to source their supplies.

I feel many beginners aren't being taught that they have everything they need without spending a dime. This might sound chaotic, and it is; however, witchcraft is in the heart of the witch—not in the tools or supplies. An experienced witch can get more done with a piece of paper, a pencil, and their will than an imitator can with all the supplies in a metaphysical store.

The way that I've worded that might seem like I'm "gatekeeping," but there is a difference between someone who claims to know something without ever putting in effort and someone who dedicates themselves to their spiritual path through hard work and devotion. Anyone who decides to join the path of witchcraft and wants to be a witch can! There is no prerequisite like being hereditary (being descended from a long line of witches) or coming from a particular background or race. However, what one does with that desire to truly explore and learn determines what kind of witch they will be.

A witch without any studying has no grounding to produce the energy needed to manifest their desires and will. Beginners just starting off will not know as much as an advanced witch, and that is not only okay but highly encouraged and to be expected. No one becomes an expert in anything overnight—and witchcraft is no different. There is a distinction between calling yourself a witch and truly being a witch. Witchcraft is found in the soul; it was present when you were in your spirit form, it is here now, and it will be there once this life is through.

Budget Witchcraft

Plastic witchcraft often gets confused with budget witchcraft by the pretentious, and I've noticed the intersection of these two when I am helping beginners through budget witchcraft. Budget witchcraft is not the same thing as being a plastic witch; frugal does not mean fake. Just because you're strapped for cash and using cheaper resources doesn't mean that you care any less about the earth, its resources, or the spirits that you will be working with. You are allowed to live within your means and still practice resourceful witchcraft.

Witches do not need anything in order to practice witchcraft. In a capitalist society strongly influenced by trends, it might seem as though to be a witch one would need all kinds of trappings—but there is one thing that I can swear by and that is that a witch needs nothing. Tools such as candles, jars, bells, and incense are used to focus and raise energy, but they are not essential. When a beginner is just starting out in their journey, tools such as these aid in learning how to focus intention and manifest the witch's will.

When you are just starting out, it might feel overwhelming figuring out what is "right." It might seem as though you need a book of shadows, or an altar, or any number of other things. While I don't discourage acquiring these things eventually, you really only need two things to start: a dedicated space for focusing your energy and a notebook to write things down so you don't forget. The earth is an altar for all its children, free of charge and abundant in space. And walking outside on a nice day is as soul-satisfying as building and cleaning an altar for a god or ancestor.

Some of the "necessary" basic supplies are the easiest to source. I say necessary because there are certain tools that help us progress in our growth; however what is necessary to me might not be necessary to the next witch. In that list of essential tools is a book of shadows or what is commonly referred to as a grimoire. Both of these terms are fancy ways to describe a spellbook. A book of shadows is a personal book of spells, notes, and rituals feeling very similar to a journal but a little more formal. This is a Wiccan term and not every witch keeps a book of shadows. Similarly, a grimoire is a formal book of spells and useful information that is often passed down in lineage or shared by a coven or group of witches. Not every witch keeps a grimoire.

Personally, I like to keep a physical journal and digital notes. I use the note section in my phone that backs up to my email account to store all of my book of shadow/grimoire/magickal entries. I organize this and keep it as a much more accessible resource for quick reference throughout my day. In my spare time, I use a paper journal to write notes on books and my various thoughts. In this way, I have created a practice that is both sustainable to me as an individual witch and useful. I don't write things in these books that can be easily looked up online, such as moon phases or color correspondences. I can pull any number of books off my shelves or do a five-second search to get the answer. I write about my thoughts and feelings when I read things or how I interpret the energy of particular things such as moon phases. A witchcraft journal/book of shadows/grimoire can be literally whatever you want it to be!

In witchcraft, like in everything else, live within your means. Even if those means are conventional. Bought something in plastic? Reuse it or recycle it. Ended up in the fast fashion cycle for whatever reason? Repair it instead of throwing it away. Don't forget that fast fashion is some of the only fashion for certain sizes. Taking care of yourself financially goes hand in hand with taking care of your mental and spiritual health. Don't allow anyone's opinion about what a witch "should" be make you feel lesser-than for living within your means. You don't have to be anyone's flavor but your own.

Altar Basics

Altars are important to most witches, and each one is as individual as a book of shadows or grimoire! I am a folk witch, and my altars reflect that. In many books on Wicca, you will find detailed instructions on what tools you should have to build your altar, where it should be placed, and what should be on it. In *The Spiral Dance*, Starhawk describes the altar this way:

> *The tools [of a coven] are usually kept on an altar, which may be anything from a hand-carved antique chest to a box covered with a cloth. When used for regular meditation and magical practice, the altar becomes charged with energy, a vortex of power. Generally, a Witch's altar faces north, and the tools are placed in their corresponding directions. Images of the Goddess and God—statues, shells, seeds, flowers, or a minor—take a central position.*

Personally, and as a folk witch, this is not how I work with altars at all. In folk witchcraft, you make an altar where you're guided to with the materials you are guided to. I'd like to mention that there is absolutely nothing wrong with creating a more ritual-based altar. This works for some witches and allows them to truly focus their energy in ways that they wouldn't be able to with the chaos that is a natural folk altar. However, this is one of the most time-tested and accessible methods of creating an altar, in my opinion. Additionally, using a more folk-based method versus ritualist method allows for the moving pieces of the altar to ebb and flow with the changing of the season.

So how do you make such an altar? Well I'm glad you asked! First, allow yourself to release the idea of what an altar "should" be and what should be on it. Think about your space and your purpose. Are you creating an altar to celebrate a season? Are you creating an altar for a deity? Are you creating a working altar to handle all of those topics and more? Once you have identified *why* you are making your altar, the fun truly begins.

Let's identify a few common altars and how you would make them— travel altars for roaming and closeted witches, seasonal altars, and a general working altar. While there are many types of altars, mastering these three makes it easier to create any other kind of altar to suit your needs.

There are a few questions you need to ask yourself before you start building any kind of altar:

What is important to me?

What items can I incorporate or symbolize that?

Do I need lots of space or a little space?

Do I want to stand or sit at my altar?

Will any of the items I choose need to be routinely changed out?

Your answers will be unique to you and you alone, and they may change as time goes on and your needs and interests evolve.

Travel Altars

Travel altars are typically miniature versions of a general working altar. They allow the witch to connect back and ground themselves for their spiritual practice no matter where they are. Common items in travel altars include mini pencils (like the kind from IKEA), a piece or two of paper, matches or a small lighter, a birthday candle, a small crystal (typically quartz), bagged herbs, and a pendant of some kind. These travel altars are typically held in a candy or mint tin, but have occasionally been seen in larger containers such as shoeboxes if it is just a working altar for a closeted witch.

I like to pack my travel altar in a makeup bag I got out of the dollar bin at Target. Included in it are the following items: a mini Polaroid picture, a lighter, cone incense, a tealight candle, salt packets, and a quartz angel statue. Also, while it's not technically in my travel altar, I always carry a deck of tarot cards in my purse or backpack. There is no right or wrong way to make a travel altar, and they're superfun to assemble!

Seasonal Altars

There are two primary ways to make a seasonal altar: indoors or outdoors. I think that creating a seasonal altar outdoors lends an extra element of connection with the energy of the earth, but I also recognize that this is not always feasible or accessible for every witch. If an outdoor altar is possible for you, wonderful! If it isn't, and indoor altar will work just fine. Seasonal altars can be made to celebrate the literal season, or they can be made and changed with each turn of the wheel.

Outdoor Altars

When creating an outdoor seasonal altar, start by closing your eyes and allowing the energy of your surroundings to flow through you. Where are you called to place this altar? When you find the spot, look around. Are there any rocks or pieces of wood or naturally carved-out spots that seem like natural places for an altar? If this is a temporary altar that you will be packing up when you leave, you can use any supplies that you brought in, such as tables, cloths, statues, candles, etc. If you are crafting a more permanent altar to last through the season that you can return to again and again, it is best to use the material that nature has supplied to prevent damage to the space you are in.

Indoor Altars

When creating an indoor altar, all bets on decoration are off! I recommend setting up a seasonal altar in or near a windowsill that faces east or west. That way this can be a place of peace and reflection during either the birth or death of the day. Currently, I have a seasonal altar that is mounted to the wall with my windowsill. Your materials and the size of the altar will depend on what you'll use the altar for—general seasonal offerings, sabbats, or a mix of seasons.

For me, this altar only acknowledges the four major seasons—autumn, winter, spring, and summer—plus Samhain and Yule. It is decorated with fresh seasonal flowers, seven-day prayer candles that match the season (black or orange in autumn, red or blue in winter, pink or green in spring, and red or yellow in summer), art from various pagan artists depicting gods and goddesses, a grapevine pentacle, and typically books. This is not an altar where I specifically petition for things, so unless I am working on an active spell, there aren't any offerings since it is in a common area of my house and I have pets.

General Working Altars

Working altars are typically extremely anti-aesthetic and hidden in a private area of the home. They are what most people assume a witch's altar is, based on fiction. This type of altar is typically built on a shelf, desk, or table and may include items such as books, journals, chalices, athame, crystals, candles, statues, photos, money, trinkets, offerings, or decorations. This is a place where a witch can come to connect with their ancestors, guides, higher powers, and themselves. The work done on these altars can be introspective (shadow work), productive (manifestations), or baneful in nature.

Working altars do require the most maintenance out of the various types of altars we have gone over. They need to be cleaned regularly to show respect to ourselves and the spirits we work with. Perishable offerings need to be changed and replenished often. Candles need to be replaced when they have run their course, and spellwork needs to be disposed of.

As a side note, one of the most common questions that beginner witches have when first starting out is to find out what to do with spell remains. There are various ways to dispose of a spell once it is finished with at your altar. You can bury it, leave it at a crossroads, or throw it away. Depending on the type of spell, you might consider doing one of the first options before you choose the trash, as there is a good chance you will not want those spell remains lingering around your house or property for any prolonged period of time.

To sum it all up, an altar is what you make of it. Christians refer to their body as a "temple," and this thought isn't necessarily wrong. No matter where you are, the connection to spirit is there with you. All you have to do is reach out!

Manifestation/Abundance

If you're a budget witch, you understand the importance of a good abundance manifestation without needing to be told. I've been working with and modifying my bare-bones abundance ritual for years now and have found that this budget-friendly setup is good for the wallet while maintaining the integrity of the magick.

When we manifest anything, it is because we are looking to gain or change something. Manifesting abundance is no different, except that it requires us to look at what we already have been blessed with before we will be given more. If you come from a place of me, me, me, your abundance rituals will always fail. Abundance requires us to see, appreciate, and be grateful for the things we are blessed to have before we will be given more. In this way, receiving an abundance is a lot like a thanksgiving. We bless ourselves with more blessings and allow the universe to bestow additional blessings on top.

SIMPLE ABUNDANCE RITUAL

Simplified rituals are some of the most powerful and abundant rituals that there are. They are a reminder for witches of every level that we really can change our reality with little more than the power of our mind.

You will need:

- **Your imagination**
- **A pen and paper**
- **A candle (optional)**
- **Your altar!**

Before beginning any ritual, I like to take a few minutes to quiet my mind and focus. Meditation opens your mind to accept your spirit and merges your conscious mind with your subconscious mind. Allow yourself about ten minutes to focus and center. This will ensure that you have the proper attention to create what you are trying to manifest, and it allows your mind and spirit to reset from being digitally and physically connected to anything other than the intentions you are about to set.

After calming your mind and calling in your energy and spirit, it is time to focus that energy. The easiest way to do this is by lighting a candle.

Under the light of the candle, with a reset and focused energy, visualize all of the abundance currently in your life. Abundance could look like a stocked pantry, a living room full of friends and family, a college degree, a library full of resources. Write down each of your abundances individually. Once you've completed the list, one at a time, say each blessing out loud. Thank the universe for the blessings in your life, and burn the list in the candle's flame.

Next, you will manifest future abundance. This part is especially important to stay focused for. Do not allow doubts and fears to gain traction as you work through the visualization of your future. Fear has no place here.

Close your eyes and visualize what abundance will look like in your life. Wealth? Health? Family? Career? Whatever it is, visualize yourself in it. What are you doing? How do you feel? How did you get there? The more vivid your manifestation, the more powerful it will be.

Once you are done visualizing this abundance, write the scene on a piece of paper, beginning with the phrase "I am." For example,

"I am surrounded by an abundance of friends who support me."

"I am financially self-sufficient and comfortable in my lifestyle."

Next, fold the paper three times and set it in the flames. As it burns, close your eyes and continue to visualize your manifestation.

If you aren't using any tools, you can visualize a candle in your mind's eye and keep a mental list of your blessings. Allow the images of your blessings to approach and vanish with the flame when the times comes. Again, if you are only visualizing this blessing, allow the images to approach the candle in your mind until they vanish.

6

THE SPIRITUAL GARDEN

*Your garden, regardless of the form it takes, is the visible symbol of your
commitment to making room for the spirit in everyday life.*

—Peg Streep, *Spiritual Gardening*

I have always thought that a garden is the perfect metaphor for life. Nearly every part of the garden can reflect the various stages of our physical, emotional, intellectual, and spiritual lives. On a physical level, gardens are typically started by seed (or bulb), and the seed germinates and grows. As time goes on, the seed becomes a plant, the plant produces and reproduces, and eventually it dies or goes into a reduced state for winter. However, I find that gardens really reverberate with humans when we look at them on an emotional and intellectual level.

Emotionally, intellectually, and spiritually, we grow from seed. We are on a quest to grow, to thrive, and we seek the sun. We chase what sustains us, and sometimes we have some bumps along the way. With neglect, it is all too easy for our gardens to become overgrown with weeds. These weeds can look like negative habits, toxic surroundings, self-hate, or doubt. Weeds, when left unchecked, can overtake a once thriving and beautiful garden.

The weeds of negativity are not easy to tame! There is a very real and prevalent spiritually bypassing dialogue in the witchcraft community that says there is no room for negativity. We need to be love and light 24/7. However, those of us who are grounded know this is neither possible nor healthy. A healthy mind stays rooted in what is real and processes one's thoughts and feelings without the lens of guilt that "love and light" often brings with it. Weeding the garden of our soul is time-consuming, hard, and absolutely worth the effort.

Soul Planting

Gardening to the witch should not be purely a physical experience but a soul-deep interaction. It is where we give ourselves freely to the earth, and the earth gives itself, its bounty, and its energy back to us. In this way, the relationship between the gardener and their garden is much more spiritually tuned. Including our garden in our daily spiritual practice takes it out of the realm of chores and puts it into the realm of enlightenment.

Before you begin working on planning and planting, you will need to take a good look at what your overall goals are for your garden. Well-tended gardens become a sacred space, a place where one can retreat from the noise and pressure of technology and daily life. When you think about your garden, what images come to mind? Do you see tons of bright flowers? Vegetables and fruits? Or lots of lettuces and herbs?

If you don't have a green thumb or the ideal gardening space, don't worry. There are going to be times when for a variety of reasons you can't have a traditional garden, or perhaps you live in an apartment and only have access to a patio. I have been gardening for more than ten years and have found some techniques that really work for all types of gardening. And no matter the size of the space, someone who is dedicated to growing can truly flourish no matter the situation if they put their mind to it.

Regardless of size, space, or climate, every witch has the ability to make their own little sanctuary. Whether you have a windowsill, a patio, a backyard, or acres, you are able to make any space your own. When planning for a spiritual garden, there are some important factors that will help you build and grow your space in a conscious and sustainable manner.

Planning

When you're first setting out a plan, grab a notebook to write down notes for current and future use. To begin, where do you think you could grow your garden? Physically go to that space and see how you feel in it. While you are there, take a look at where the sun is in relation to the time and where you would want to put your plants.

The sun has a large role in the overall success of a witch's garden. Too much or too little sunlight could stunt the growth of an otherwise healthy plant. Taking the morning, noon, and afternoon sun into consideration, as well as where the shade hits for microclimates, will allow for a better planned witch's garden. Are there any existing plants where you want to grow your garden? Would you want to incorporate these plants or remove or relocate them?

Most importantly, consider which element your spirit connects to the most. With which element do you feel most confident and comfortable? This is important because it can help determine what kind of garden you build and how you build it in order to invoke certain elements. For example, I am drawn to fire, so I plant a lot of red, orange, and yellow flowers to invoke warmth and passion.

Next, decide what type of garden to build and grow for your life and spirit. There are many options, such as a tranquility garden if you feel as though you are often overstimulated. There are healing gardens, where you can grow herbs for the physical and spiritual body. Or perhaps a meditation garden, were you could go at any time of the day and just sit. Additionally, you can have a god or goddess garden that connects to the spirits of the land, your ancestors, your guides, and your gods. There are also aromatherapy gardens, which have different plants for the purposes of creating incense and resins. This type of garden has proved especially useful to me personally, as I connect to it in its practical uses for spiritual and mental health purposes.

It's important to decide early on whether you're going to plant in the ground or in containers. Each method has its benefits and complications, but at the end of the day a successful garden comes down to working with what you've got versus against it. Let's start with container gardening, because it's the easiest and most accessible way to garden for the modern witch. You can have a successful container garden without purchasing expensive supplies or relying on good weather and ground conditions.

Container Gardens

There are tons of containers that you can turn into pots—but it's important to make sure that whatever you choose has proper drainage. Closed-bottom pots are known to cause many issues, such as poor drainage and root rot. The leading cause of root rot with indoor plants has everything to do with overwatering and using closed-bottom pots.

I love using old yogurt containers and egg cartons to start my seeds indoors because they are small and easy to replant. I tend to get my eggs at Trader Joe's, which have containers that are for the most part biodegradable so I don't have to worry about pulling my little seedling out of its container prematurely. It is important to think about future transplanting, because if seedlings are moved too early it may shock them, which could cause death.

I like to leave my containers outdoors whenever possible for direct sun exposure as well as fresh air and rainwater. Living in South Florida, we get a lot of rain, which is awesome but also somewhat stressful for planting conditions. There is not only humidity but also rain, leading to moist soil conditions. This is another instance where good drainage is key to plant health.

Another positive benefit of container gardening is that you don't actually have to work with this season that you're in. While I do highly recommend gardening intuitively based on the season around you, I recognize that that might not always be possible. Growing your plants in containers allows you to garden during more extreme conditions, such as deep winter or deep summer.

All of the best plants for witchcraft can be grown through containers exclusively, regardless of season. Starting your herbs from seed that you've grown yourself not only allows your energy and magick to touch the plants that you're going to be using, but it allows your magick to transcend levels through your spellwork that you did not even know you could reach.

Outdoor Gardening

When planning your outdoor garden, the most important factor is your specific climate. Different regions have different climates, so it's important to dive deeper than just the four basic seasons. Plants also have different needs for sun, water, shade, soil, and nutrients.

The easiest way to learn about your specific climate, and determine which plants will thrive there, is to look up your hardiness zone. Hardiness zones were developed by the United States Department of Agriculture (USDA) and include thirteen zones that range by a temperature scale. Throughout the years, other hardiness schemes have been developed and adopted for other parts of the globe, but the USDA scale is the most common.

Equally important to planning a successful outdoor garden is looking at various environmental factors, including soil type, soil moisture and drainage, humidity, nutrients, light, temperature, and duration of exposure to extreme heat or cold.

When it is time to sit down and plan an outdoor garden sanctuary, it is a good idea to look back at your earlier notes about your ideas, senses, and elemental preferences. Then it is time to decide a method of attack that is not only effective but efficient. Do you want to start from seed or seedling? If from seed, are you starting indoors in accordance with your zone or are you waiting late enough into the season to avoid frost for direct sowing?

Personally, I grow a small garden in my patio and front walkway. The number of plants I keep is fairly small, so I tend to buy seedlings that have been started already. There are two main reasons for this: first, they are more economical, and second, a seedling already has a leg up, with a healthy start from the nursery.

Take a look at all of the plants you would like to grow this season. On the back of the seed packet make sure to review the sun, soil, and watering requirements. If a plant calls for partial shade, it is typically a good idea to give morning sun versus afternoon sun, as the afternoon sun can often be too harsh for sensitive plants.

Looking through the requirements, you get to make the choice of surface planting, raised-bed planting, hill planting, or mound planting. If you decide to go with surface planting methods, you can choose between single, double, or any type of row planting scheme that your heart desires. As a word of wisdom, it is easier to maintain and care for two shorter rows rather than a single long, continuous one. Surface planting with rows is probably the quickest and easiest method for a new gardener and requires little expertise. Plant the seeds directly into the soil after the last frost, then weed, water, and watch your garden grow!

Practical Intuition in the Garden

Earlier, we went over the practical applications of intuition, but the garden is one of the most useful places to pull out that intuitive tool kit. Plants can be tricky, and every now and again everyone has questions and doubts. Did I overwater? Underwater? Are my plants lacking nutrition? How can I keep pests from eating my plants? The practical use of our intuition is not only necessary, it is required. There is no time more relevant for the practical use of intuition.

Through time, practice, and trial and error, you will learn what works and what does not. In spiritual gardening, it is important to use the tools your intuition is calling for. Don't worry about what anyone in real life or on the internet has to say—follow your guides for your individual path and space. The more you pay attention to this, the sooner your crafted space will manifest before your eyes.

Correspondence Building .

When first beginning to use plants and herbs magickly, it is common to lean on literature for guidance. You could do a quick search and find information on tons of common plants or go to the library or local bookstore and check out books on green witchcraft. However, what these books don't teach you is how to figure out that information for yourself.

Say you come across a plant, search for it, and see that no correspondences have been written about it. You wonder, Can this be used magickly? The answer is a resounding yes! Just because you can't find an "official" source on the magickal uses for a particular plant doesn't mean that it doesn't serve a purpose both practically and magickly. The internet is not the be-all and end-all of witchcraft, nor it is the endpoint of information for our journey.

There are a few things to look at when you first start to decode a plant (or any material for magickal use, really). The basics to this theory are that the witch follows a set of general guidelines to get them to the point of understanding. There's a checklist I like to use when I start working with a new plant or material.

CORRESPONDENCE CHECKLIST

- **Name of material:**
- **Size:**
- **Color:**
- **Where to get it:**
- **Plant questions:**

  What type of plant is it (family, genus)?

  Is it poisonous? (Research this answer if you aren't certain.)

  Is it native?

  Is it edible? (Research this answer if you aren't certain.)

  Is it flowering?

  How healthy does it appear to be?

  How is it used? (Possible uses could include medicinal, food, cleaning.)

  How is it used magickly?

  How will I use it magickly?

  How do I feel when I'm working with it?

By answering a few basic questions—as many as you can—you'll get a good feeling for the plant or material before you start working with it. This knowledge will allow you to intuitively use materials that benefit and strengthen your overall goal.

Let's work through a few examples of how to use this basic correspondence building technique. First off is cannabis, my most requested plant from students. We'll also take a look at snapdragons and sponge gourds. Neither really has a lot written on them, but there's so much we can do with them that they're useful as examples of underdog plant potential.

Cannabis

Believe it or not, the most common plant that I get requested to go through for magickal purposes by my students is actually cannabis. I am not a cannabis user, but I do know quite a bit about the plant, so finding its properties for a spiritual purpose was actually pretty easy. In this regard, spiritual purpose is referring to external, ritual-based uses, not recreational or medicinal use.

Most of us understand what cannabis is and what it does. It has recreational, commercial, and medicinal purposes and is quite popular. To look at the plant, you would really be considering the different varieties: *Cannabis sativa, Cannabis indica, Cannabis ruderalis,* and hybrids of these.

Let's take a look at the family tree to start. We can see that cannabis is actually part of the rose family. This basic information gives a pretty big lead about the uses for this plant. While a lot of people assume that cannabis would have applications in protection spells, this plant is actually better suited for other purposes. Cannabis is also related to hops (as in beer), elm (hackberry), and figs (distantly). We know that hops are good for health and wellness spells, as well as dream work. (It's also been said that hops is a good anti-aphrodisiac, but I don't know how accurate that is.) Elm is well known in love and fertility spellwork. And figs are used for divination, prosperity, fertility, and love.

Knowing that cannabis is in the Rosales order, meaning that it is directly related to roses, is a pretty good first indicator that this plant has strength in love and healing. This does not necessarily mean romantic love but can also mean self-love as well. Cannabis is also a potent medicine, used to solve various ailments throughout history. In today's world, cannabis is a hot topic, with people on both sides of the fence. Whether you use it in your spiritual craft or not is your personal choice.

After looking at the related plants and how they are used, it is time to examine the actual plant in question. Start from the roots and work your way up. What does it look like, and what does it smell like? These are both pretty obvious questions, but it's good to know whether the roots are long and deep, or spread out like a big tree. Also make sure to take note of the overall health of the plant. It's best to only work with healthy plants that have the extra energy to lend us in our magick.

Each plant has different strengths than the other varieties. For example, take a simple rose. One could give a yellow rose to a friend and a red rose to their partner or lover. Different variations of plants all have different strengths and weaknesses, and plants like cannabis are no different.

Snapdragons

Snapdragons are easily one of the coolest types of flowers. Not only do they have a beautiful bloom, but when they die, the husks of their flowers look like little skulls. Snapdragons self-seed, dropping seeds from the skulls of the flowers that came before. I've personally never had an issue with them coming back in my garden every year.

There are some important features to take note of before you start looking at the actual family order of this plant. These are tenacious, beautiful plants. They show both life and death within their flowers and are equally balanced in both ways.

Looking at the family tree of snapdragons shows us that they are relatives of the foxglove. Foxgloves are common in magickal practice, but they require extra care because they are highly toxic. Foxgloves are closely related to fairy lore but have also been used in shadow work and intuition. Due to its toxicity this plant cannot be ingested, and it is not good to handle frequently (but it is useful magickly). During Beltane, when the wall between our world and the fae is thinner, foxglove makes a great offering.

Snapdragons, on the other hand, are not poisonous—so they are a lot easier to work with and can be used more universally. Snapdragons can be used year-round for altars and offerings and can be used to symbolize life or death, depending on the face of the planet. If the flowers are blooming, they make a great altar offering and decoration. If the flowers have died and you're left with the dried skulls of the husk, snapdragons become the perfect Samhain altar offering.

Sponge Gourds

Last but not least is the sponge gourd. This might seem like a random choice, and honestly it kind of is. Here is my sponge gourd story: I accidentally ordered a ton of seeds for sponge gourds one year and was left with a bunch of plants that I didn't really know how to care for. I didn't know how to use them, and I didn't know if they had any real purpose aside from making a bunch of zucchini-looking plants that you can't actually eat.

What I learned, however, is that every plant has its purpose. The vines and leaves on the sponge gourd are some of the most breathtaking

I've ever seen. They grew along my fence line, completely enclosed my garden, and made it look like the most beautiful fairy space I've ever seen. On top of that, they produce beautiful flowers.

Sponge gourds are related to other gourd and melon plants such as cucumbers and watermelons. Cucumbers are used in healing and fertility work, and watermelons are used for growth, fertility, lust, and peace. What separates sponge gourds from these other gourds, however, is that sponge gourds are inedible. Their primary function is as literal cleaning sponges made from the dried gourd. This shows that its practical and magickal use most likely lies in the hearth and home. Bring sponge gourds inside to dry to promote prosperity and fertility throughout your household.

While many correspondences have been written, rewritten, and cross-examined, there are so many wonderful plants out there just waiting for you to notice them. Each of us lives in a unique place, surrounded by unique flora. Challenge yourself to branch away from plants with common associations and see what you can get into!

7

LOCAL ELEMENTS
AND SPIRITS

We abuse land because we regard it as a commodity belonging to us. When we see land as a community to which we belong, we may begin to use it with love and respect.

—Aldo Leopold

The 1997 film *Princess Mononoke* by Hayao Miyazaki is one of the most impactful movies on the concept of local elements and land spirits that has ever been created. This epic fantasy focuses on the ongoing struggle between nature and human influence. If you haven't watched this film, take note—because now you have homework. I highly recommend this film to all of my students to better grasp the theory of local elements and spiritual empathy.

Land spirits are not specific to any particular culture. Throughout history, every culture has held some type of belief relating to the spirits of the land and the creatures that inhabit it. Native American, Irish, Norse, Germanic tribes, Indian, Chinese, and Japanese all held land spirits in special esteem.

The line between what makes one entity a spirit of the land and another entity a god can be somewhat blurry. Land spirits can also be mistaken for mythological creatures, such as faeries. Spirits of the land can be land gods and rule over the lands that they reside on, or they can be literal attachments to particular features in the land. There are forest spirits, lake and river spirits, plain spirits, rock and mountain spirits.

As land becomes developed, the neighborhoods and cities gain spirits as well. Just because a house is built on land doesn't mean the house isn't part of that living land anymore. Structures not only reside within the spirit of the land, but through time develop their own unique spirits as well.

Understanding Land and Nature Spirits

To understand land spirits, you need to first understand the land and space that you inhabit. What type of land was your property on before it was developed? What types of nature reside there now? How many trees are around you, and what is their general health? As you step outside, do you feel the spirits of nature flow around you freely, or do they feel stagnant and lazy?

I live in a part of South Florida that was once part of the Everglades. Much of South Florida was drained and then built in, allowing for development further west. The natural spirits of the land I live on are swampy, yet have adapted to meet the growing urban culture. Additionally, Florida sits on top of a limestone platform. According to a University of Florida Department of Wildlife Ecology and Conservation article, during the last Ice Age, sea levels were much lower and exposed more of the Florida coastline. Much of the exposed land became savanna in nature, which is a grassy tropical or subtropical plain with few trees. This savanna is still seen today! Every land has its own unique history waiting to be uncovered. Researching the geological aspects of the lands that we live on allows us to better understand and connect with the spirits that reside there as well.

Nature spirits have roles outside of human understanding and logic. They don't exist in such an obtrusive way that humans are aware of them, yet they work diligently nonetheless. Nature spirits and land spirits help protect the land and the creatures that reside on it. When people talk about hauntings of new structures, and even some older structures, what they are really dealing with is confused land spirits. When people build on land without acknowledging the other creatures, they displace not only plants and animals but spirits as well. Sometimes, these spirits stay on the land and try to rebuild and protect what they can. Sometimes, these spirits are angry, lost, and confused.

The same thing happens in older structures when new owners take over. A new owner might come into an older house and decide that the house is "haunted," when really the spirits that reside there are confused. These spirits may feel as though their space is being encroached upon by a person who didn't have the decency to introduce themselves and make their intentions known. Flowing with the harmony of the spirits that are already present can solve the issues of land and structure disturbances nearly every time they come up.

Connecting with Your Land Spirits

Working with and creating a relationship with land, nature, and structure spirits is a wholly intuitive practice. An understanding doesn't typically happen overnight; but when we work on strengthening our intuitive skills, it is something that can easily be accomplished by any witch, regardless of overall skill level.

When I lived in Montana, one of my teachers told me that on every property there is one spirit in charge of balancing the rest. At the time, this was the spirit of a beautiful old weeping willow tree on the property between our garden and house. This old tree stood watch over the property, and kept all the various people, pets, plants, and spirits that inhabited it safe. I am certain that this tree took the negativity from some of the people on the property and filtered it back out in a way that could be managed. It was under the wisdom of this tree that I first became spiritually aware as an adult.

In my current house, this spirit is actually a three-hundred-pound limestone boulder. The garden around it teems with the beauty of life, flowers, and butterflies. The garden is stable and safe because the spirit of the boulder grounds it. The boulder spirit of my yard has helped protect me many times. During Hurricane Irma, the large oak tree above the roof of my room broke and collapsed. Instead of coming through the roof, the branch fell limb-end first, scraping my window but leaving the structure in one piece. At the time, I could literally feel the energy of protection radiating around my space.

Every property has a primary guardian spirit, whether that is a tree, boulder, river, well, or any other element. Building a relationship with this spirit is the most important part of working with your local land spirits.

FIND YOUR PRIMARY GUARDIAN SPIRIT

When you are ready to begin building this relationship, step outdoors and sit in a way where your skin comes in direct contact with the natural ground. Close your eyes and visualize the property, as if you were floating above it and looking down. See each element as it truly is: where the buildings meet the trees, where the sun and shade hit the plants and soil, where there might be strength or sickness in the land itself. Open up your intuition as you are looking down. Can you identify the source of the primary land spirit?

When you are able to identify the spirit of land, introduce yourself. In your mind, visualize what this spirit might look or sound like. Giving the spirit an association will allow you to build a relationship and connection with them. The more you honor and work with this entity, the stronger your bond will become.

Land and Ancestry

All witches have a place of origin. This place ties our living blood with the living land and spirit of a particular place. Our magick is more easily focused in these places and connects freely with the spirits of nature. Throughout the course of history, people have moved away from their lands either by choice or by force. Humans are flexible, adaptable, and forward-thinking. However, like plants, when we are separated from our roots, we begin to wither.

The topic of ancestor work often sparks questions for people who do not know where exactly they came from. Not everyone is blessed to come from a line of people who definitively knew who they were and where they originated. While some people have a family Bible passed down through generations, keeping track of who came when, others have just heard word of mouth things such as, "I think your grandmother came from ____ ."

This tends to be primarily an American problem. People have immigrated all over the globe from various places, but no place is as much of a melting pot as modern-day America. For those who don't know where their family comes from, it's easy to claim, "I'm an American"; but what is an American really? A blend of cultures? A dark history built on the backs of other cultures. Is it perhaps a more modern interpretation of immigrants choosing to come over in recent years?

As modern technology has advanced, genetic tests like those by National Geographic and ancestry.com have offered a solution. Using these tests is as simple as paying for them, sending in some DNA, and waiting for your results. Even growing up fortunate enough to know exactly where my blood comes from, I decided to take an ancestry DNA test a few years ago. In my experience, the test was completely accurate, giving me the exact results I was expecting, but specifying how much of what came from where.

It should be noted that taking a DNA test and learning you're 1 to 5 percent of anything doesn't give a person free rein to appropriate that culture or those people. For ancestry that ranges from 1 to 5 percent, that would mean the ancestor was most likely between six and eight generations away from you today. The energy of that culture is in your blood, but it is not the dominant factor in your current ancestry. These cultures should be treated with respect and reverence as you build the connection over time. In my own ancestry, there is just over 70 percent Irish/Scottish/Welsh, with 2 percent Spanish. I'm not sure when this occurred in my tree, but I feel fairly confident in the assumption that I am not in fact Spanish at all but that somehow that small piece was related to the Gauls, who were a Celtic people.

Over the years, ancestor magick has become bigger and bigger in the witchcraft community. I rely heavily on my ancestors in my personal craft. Ancestor magick is more than just connecting to your ancestors— it is connecting to the spirit of yourself, your blood, the energy of your physical body, and the land. What this means is that it's not simply your ancestors, but everything that envelops them.

Someone who has Irish ancestry is going to have a different connection to the land than someone with Native American ancestry, or Russian ancestry. These ancestors connected to the land and the local spirits in a way that connects our blood to that same land and those same local spirits. It's important to recognize where you are and where you came from when working with your ancestors in their magick. Sometimes it might feel a little silly if you aren't sure of pronunciation, but it is a good practice to incorporate the native tongue of your ancestors into your magick when working with them. Your ancestors will recognize your spirit and your intent, but they will always have an easier time relating to what was familiar to them.

This is not to say that you have to learn a foreign language to perform this kind of magick. But you can pick up a few words here and there and incorporate them into your spells and rituals. The modern Irish language is such a mix of different influences that I'm pretty sure my ancient ancestors wouldn't really understand it. But what I can do for them is incorporate some of the gods that they knew, some of the written language and the music of the land. I can also include the land, the dirt, the trees, the water, and the essence of the land that they inhabited when they were here.

Connecting this piece to our magick is especially important for Americans who do not claim Native American ancestry, which is the majority of us. Your ancestors are not going to have the same connection to this land as they would if they were native. Going back to the roots of our culture, even if we were not raised with those roots, we can help create a spiritual depth and bond between our spirit and our flesh. Learning about and participating in the traditions of your ancestral heritage will strengthen the connection for your ancestral and blood magick.

Blood Magick

Blood magick is one of those things that has been closely guarded by those who practice it and shunned by those in the witchcraft community who do not understand it. If someone were to mention "blood magick," you might think of sacrifice or sex magick—but I promise that is not all it is. Blood magick both invokes and evokes the bond between the "heavens" and the earth, where spirit meets flesh. It is our most primal form of magick, and our most powerful tool.

Blood is the sustainer of all life and the creator of death. While blood doesn't *actually* create death, it understands the duality better than any other piece of our physical body. Remember, you are not just a body, but a spirit within a body. After this life is over, what will you have to show for it? Our blood is a sacred source of magick. We are unable to exist without it, and problems in our blood cause decay of the physical, mental, and spiritual bodies we own as well. While we are in the flesh, our spirit is joined with our physical body. It is necessary to take care of each element of life in order to feely work with the magick harnessed within our DNA.

I've heard over and over again through the years that blood magick is "dangerous" or "evil." I don't think anything that comes from our own bodies can inherently be evil. I am also not of the opinion that the use of my blood makes me any more vulnerable for a psychic or spiritual attack. If that were the case, I would have to be concerned about the amount of hair I am constantly shedding or coughing/sneezing during a ritual.

While I feel as though I use blood magick a little more liberally than many modern witches in regular practice, I had the unique experience to dedicate myself to my god in a place of spiritual significance recently. I was in Ireland with my partner for a wedding, and our route to the venue took us through my family's ancestral lands. The second we crossed into that territory, I could feel the energy within myself begin to shift. This was the first time I decided to dedicate myself in blood to my calling as a witch.

I have been practicing my American Irish folk-based craft since 2001. My mother was an Irish Catholic folk practitioner, and everything I know I learned from the basic principles she taught me. Eighteen years later, after multiple trips to Ireland, I was finally visiting where my family had lived for hundreds of years. At a random point on the side of a little Irish highway, in hills that probably have no modern name or significance, I reclaimed myself as a witch.

Two days later, we were packing up to leave and come back to America. We had about twenty-four hours before our 4:00 a.m. flight and nothing to do for the day. I had been feeling a strange calling throughout the trip to visit the sea. Not only did I go out of my way to visit it in Dublin, we visited it in Galway and Northern Ireland as well. I had recently accepted Manannán Mac Lir ("son of the sea") as my primary god and felt as though he was trying to tell me something.

So with a few hours and a rental car, I convinced my party that we should drive from Dublin to the Giant's Causeway on the coast of Northern Ireland and then back for our 4:00 a.m. flight. Thankfully, they obliged and we got there just as the sun was beginning to set. Among the rocks and in the presence of Manannán Mac Lir, I reclaimed myself as a witch. I walked alone down among the rocks to a small mossy area that was as much part of the land as it was the sea. I made a small cut on my finger with a pin and said out loud:

> *Between sand and sulfur,*
> *Stone and sea,*
> *This blood, I give,*
> *For all time, and to thee.*

I wasn't sure what I was expecting to happen, but what did happen fundamentally changed the way I view and practice my personal craft. A large bird flew by and landed a few stones over. It made this loud calling sound, which was answered by other birds. Up until this point the causeway had been completely quiet, with only me and probably five other people (all photographers) spread throughout it. This is the moment I was reborn.

If you haven't found a god to devote yourself to or are not sure how to find one, don't fret. After eighteen years of working toward my personal path of witchcraft, I only came into contact with the god that I would devote myself to by accident.

My recommendation for those still searching for a deity is to close your eyes and imagine the place you feel most at peace. Where do you feel whole? What are you doing? For me, this place has always been on a boat or by the beach. It took me eighteen years to make the connection between my safe place and the god that was drawing me to it.

Once you have realized where you feel most grounded, connected, and safe, research gods that match the description. You might be attracted to forests or mountains. You might find that you are attracted to storms or graveyards. Whatever it is that brings you a sense of fulfillment is the right place to start reaching out. While reading mythology books and studying what other witches are doing is good in theory, a book cannot offer the same feeling of fullness you experience when you have a connection to a god or goddess.

BLOOD MAGICK RITUAL

In preface to this ritual I would like to make it absolutely clear that I am not encouraging self-harm. If you feel uncomfortable using your blood, you can skip whatever parts you are uncomfortable with. Blood magick doesn't have to hurt, and I am absolutely not encouraging you to harm yourself in any way. Most gods don't typically care how you devote yourself, just that you do.

Once you have found a god, goddess, spirit, or guide to work with and are ready to dedicate yourself to your craft, assemble the following:

- **An object to make a small incision (a sterile knife or lancet is best OR, if you are experiencing your menstrual cycle, you can use this blood**
- **A candle or assortment of candles (I like to use a taper candle for the gods and goddesses, plus four seven-day jar candles: one for land spirits, one for guides, one for ancestors, and one for my spirit.)**
- **A lighter**

Light your candle(s) and stare into the flame, invoking the spirits of the land, guides, ancestors, gods, and goddesses to join you as you reclaim your right as a witch.

With your object, make a small incision on your hand, just enough to get one drop of blood. Put this blood directly into the flame and visualize your body and spirit aligning through a bright white light. As you do this, invoke the land, calling it in and thanking it for being with you on your journey. Release the land spirits back.

Focusing on the flame, invoke your personal guides and thank them for being with you on this journey. Release your guides back to the flame.

Lastly, with intention, invoke your spirit through your blood. Offer yourself to the gods and goddesses present with you. Allow yourself to be comforted into the presence of their knowledge and power. When you are ready, release your gods and goddesses and thank them for being with you.

Allow the candle to burn down completely before closing the ritual.

8

THE ORIGIN OF THE
WHEEL OF THE YEAR

Because of our traditions, we have kept our balance for many, many years. Here in Anatevka, we have traditions for everything: how to eat, how to sleep, how to wear clothes. For instance, we always keep our heads covered, and always wear a little prayer-shawl. This shows our constant devotion to God. You may ask, how did this tradition start? I'll tell you. I don't know. But it's a tradition. And because of our traditions, every one of us knows who he is, and what God expects him to do.

—Fiddler on the Roof

Throughout the course of human history, people have been using the natural cycles and rhythm of the earth to celebrate life and death, marriage and divorce, health and illness. Each season comes with its own unique celebrations and cycles within the rhythm of the year. So when did the wheel in its modern form begin to take shape?

No one specific culture can lay true claim to celebrating things such as the moon, sun, season, harvest, solstice, equinox, storm, or really any other facet of nature. It is in our very souls to celebrate, acknowledge, and give praise to the things that make us feel alive. However, each culture has its own traditions, values, and knowledge that make every named festival unique. Through time as cultures have come together, and been lost, stolen, shared, and conquered, many traditions have been made and lost and made anew.

Much of modern Western witchcraft is based off of the teachings and ideology of Aleister Crowley and the Hermetic Order of the Golden Dawn. Originally founded by a small group of English Freemasons during the late nineteenth century, the Hermetic Order of the Golden Dawn was an esoteric and occult society that had hundreds of men and women initiates.

The Order's foundations were influenced heavily by Judeo-Christian mysticism and Kabbalah, Hermeticism, ancient Egypt, Freemasonry, and alchemy, among other sources. This wide variety of foundational eclecticism helped create a tradition steeped in ceremonial and ritual-based magick. It was within this society that a way of organizing group magick and ritual came to be known. These systems were what built the foundations for what we know as modern Wicca.

This is not to say that Wicca is an offshoot of the Golden Dawn, but to point out in broader terms that the founders of Wicca (specifically

Gerald Gardner) used the skeleton of the Golden Dawn to create the methods for groupwork that we see throughout witchcraft today. The biggest, most visible reminder we have of these origins is the phrase "so mote it be," which is used widely in the right hand and Wiccan communities today. This phrase is actually Freemason in origin and was adapted by Gardner into modern Wicca.

Gerald Gardner also had a strong hand in the revival of the festivals on the modern wheel of the year. During the mid-twentieth century, Gardner adopted for his coven a wheel of the year celebrating the solstices and equinoxes as well as the four Celtic fire festivals:

Samhain (Winter Nights/Halloween/Pagan New Year)

Imbolc (Saint Brigid's Day/Candlemas)

Beltane (May Eve/May Day)

Lughnasagh (Frey Fest/Lammas)

At the time of creation, only the four Celtic holidays were named. The remaining four solstice and equinox days were described by their season and function rather than given a special name. These days were later named by Aidan Kelly in the 1970s and became popular under these names:

Yule (winter solstice)

Ostara (spring equinox)

Litha (summer solstice)

Mabon (autumn equinox)

Due to this group project of sorts with creating and naming the holidays on the wheel, we now have the mix of Celtic and Germanic-influenced holidays that we all know and love!

9

SAMHAiN

[harvest moon–first week of november
winter nights/halloween/pagan new year
first spoke on the dark side of the modern wheel of the year]

*Halloween (Samhain) starts on the first harvest moon you see in October
and ends during the first week of November.*

—Carole S.

Samhain (pronounced "sow-in") is the first festival in the wheel of the year. Also known as Halloween, All Hallow's Eve, and the Witches' New Year, Samhain is the middle point between the autumn equinox and the winter solstice. It is a multiday (and in some cases multiweek) observation that has many names and is observed in unique ways throughout various cultures. What many modern pagans and Wiccans refer to as Samhain, though, is a Celtic reconstruction from earlier, more ancient Celtic-Irish practices.

Samhain is marked by a thinner veil, reverence for the dead, and harvesting plants and livestock. The word *Samhain* means "November" in modern Irish and Scottish Gaelic, but it has been suggested that the word also takes root in the term *summer's end*. In this way, *sam*, translated from Old Irish to mean "summer," and *fuin*, meaning "end," were thrown together to form this sort of folk etymology. This, however, is just a modern theory—there is not a clear and decisive etymology to fully support this claim.

Traditionally, the Celts are believed to have split the wheel of the year into two halves. These two halves (the light half and the dark half—summer and winter) joined together and encompassed many festivals and observations, starting with Samhain. Samhain season is the first spoke on the wheel of the dark half, in good company with Yule, Imbolc, and Ostara. It is also the first of the original Celtic cross-quarter days. Samhain is the big spoke on the wheel that transitions us from the cycles of birth and growth to the cycle of death.

While celebrated by many on the night of October 31, Samhain is observed November 1. This is not a hard-and-fast rule, with many pagans celebrating in the more conglomerate harvest holiday Halloween style, which ranges from October 31 through November 5. Being a midpoint holiday, however, the actual date of Samhain does change and can be calculated by finding the day in the middle of the autumn equinox and Yule.

The Thinning Veil

One of the most common phrases we hear about Halloween and the Samhain season is that "the veil is thinning." This term has become popular in both spiritual and pop culture circles—but what does it mean? Many people believe that there is a veil that separates our world from that of the spirits. A few times a year, however, this veil becomes thin. The veil becomes noticeably thin during major holidays when deceased loved ones are remembered. That notably marks Samhain, Yule, and around the Jewish Passover/Christian Easter. Easter does tend to fall almost six months exactly from Samhain, which would make it the sister holiday on the wheel of the year.

Samhain is not the only day in which the veil is thin, but it is the period of thinning during the year of the witch. This is significant in many ways for witches who want to seriously manifest and change their lives in the new year! Think about conventional New Year's Day. How many people make wishes, resolutions, and set plans into motion? Nearly all of us! The witch's new year is a time when we can do the same exact thing, yet receive all the benefits of a thinned veil.

Messages to the Spirit World

There is a (toxic) plant called the angel trumpet. It is a flowering shrub with downward-facing flowers that hang like the ends of a trumpet. This plant has been used throughout history as a messenger to the spirit world. There is no better time than on the eve of a new year, when the veil is thin, to send a message to your ancestors! Angel trumpet plants bloom their heaviest in fall, so it is the perfect time to set your manifestations in action.

Angel trumpets have a very easy petitioning system that nearly anyone can use. It should be noted again, however, that these plants are toxic, so they should not be handled with bare hands. To send a message to the spirit world using an angel trumpet, all you need is a paper, a pen, a shovel, and an angel trumpet flower. At dawn or dusk, pick your angel trumpet flower. On your piece of paper, write exactly who you are petitioning and why. Fold this paper up and place it in the flower. To finish your petition, burry the trumpet as the sun sets or rises.

Mythology of Samhain

There is more than one amazing Irish myth regarding Samhain, from "The Adventures of Nera" to "The Wooing of Emer." It is quite notable that there is more than one story involving our Irish hero Cú Chulainn around the time of Samhain, from "The Wooing of Emer" to "The Sickbed of Cú Chulainn." These stories and epics, while no longer told around a bonfire, are still integral parts of what makes these surviving traditions grounding and unique.

What is any harvest holiday without a thanksgiving as well? The heart of Samhain is not associated with any particular deity, but encompasses all gods, goddesses, and other deities that join us during this time of thinned veil and closer connection. There are, however, some particular gods and goddesses who like to make their presence known during this time of year. This is not to say that these particular deities must be worshipped or acknowledged, but if you do happen to work with any of them, it would be a great time of year to set up a task-oriented altar.

In many Wiccan traditions, the Goddess takes the form of the triple goddess: Maiden, Mother, and Crone. This is the counterpart to the

Horned God. The literal embodiment of Samhain is the Crone. The Crone is both the last and first stage of the triple goddess. She is the last stage before death but the first stage of the matriarchy of the triple goddess and as such holds the most knowledgeable and powerful role. While there are many forms of the triple goddess, the one most widely associated with Samhain is Hecate.

Interestingly enough, Hecate is a Greek goddess yet is widely associated with the Celtic festival of Samhain. While in her Crone aspect she is the goddess of the underworld, this association is not fully why she is linked to Samhain. In *Celebrating the Seasons of Life: Samhain to Ostara*, Ashleen O'Gaea tells us, "the Romans knew her, and introduced the Celts to her when the Caesars's empire extended through Western Europe and into Britain."

At this time of year, Hecate also commonly goes by the title the Dark Goddess. The Dark Goddess is the name of the Crone embodiment of the triple goddess. Some do consider them two separate goddesses, but I believe that the Dark Goddess is the ever-growing and ever-changing goddess Hecate made modern for our modern lives. The Dark Goddess embodies mystery, the moon, the inner self, and our shadow selves. Samhain season allows us a dedicated time to appreciate, acknowledge, and work with our moon self.

Rituals of Samhain

Some of my fondest childhood memories actually revolve around the autumn holidays and specifically Samhain. My mom was an Irish folk witch, same as me, and Samhain also happened to be her favorite holiday (tied with the whole Yule season). Her wisdom that has never left me was this: "Halloween (Samhain) starts on the first harvest moon you see in October and ends during the first week of November." This has stuck with me all my adult life, and I start my Samhain rituals on the night of the first harvest moon I see in October.

This memory is the first intuitive indicator I have to begin working with my ancestors. Author Ashleen O'Gaea describes Samhain as a family reunion, and I absolutely love that analogy because it simply and succinctly cuts to the core of this festival: family, spiritual connection, thanksgiving, ending, and beginning.

Dumb Supper

The veil is thin this time of year, and our ancestors and recently lost family members are easier to contact and include in our daily lives. One of the more common Samhain traditions is what is known as a dumb supper, or a dinner with the dead. A dumb supper is a meal that not only memorializes and remembers loved ones and ancestors but also invites them back into our lives for the duration of a meal. Dumb suppers can be held any time of year and for any reason, but they are usually observed on Samhain. My Samhain celebration lasts multiple days, and I lay an ancestral place setting for each meal that we'll be celebrating, with a full food setting on the night of Samhain.

There are two main ways to perform a dumb supper. The more common, traditional way is to hold a meal in complete silence (hence the name: a dumb, or speechless, supper). This is to show reflection and respect. Typically, a meal is prepared and extra place settings are made at the table for deceased loved ones and ancestors. The meal is conducted in all seriousness, and each person considers their own private memories with those who are no longer with us.

(Don't worry about a wandering spirit joining your table—there is little to no risk of other spirits joining you at this time due to the fact that you are only inviting those of your blood.)

The second way to hold a dumb supper, and my preferred way, is what I affectionately refer to as an Irish supper. This meal is anything but quiet and ruminating. When I hold my dumb supper, I want my relatives and ancestors to feel as loved and joyful as when they were here. This version is loud, full of great food, full of alcohol, and an absolute celebration of everything that is great about being alive. This supper has three courses, and everything is handmade. (Our ancestors didn't eat Twinkies, and neither should we when we are inviting them into our homes.)

Three is the number of the Maiden, Mother, and Crone, and so serving three courses is symbolic to the spirit of the season. Similar to how American Thanksgiving always has turkey, or Christmas has a ham, my Samhain dumb supper is always based on a lamb meal. I try to use in-season, local food or produce from my garden, as opposed to out-of-season or processed foods, as much as possible.

Course 1: Homegrown creamy butternut squash soup and soda bread

Course 2: Lamb Wellington with brussels sprouts or asparagus

Course 3: Berry eton mess (berry cream parfait)

It's really not necessary that you have the same menu as me, or even have any of these items at all. What is important is that you are as authentic to your own bloodline and heritage as possible. Did any of your deceased family members eat a restricted diet? Cook for it if you can. It's not that they'll actually eat the food, but the energy and effort you put into making your guests feel comfortable counts. Just because your guests are not physically present doesn't mean you didn't invite them, and serving foods that they are used to will show respect for them in your life and home.

We can, of course, cook other dishes to go along with the deceased's favorites (and we do for our vegetarian family members). Typically, however, this is the format and menu for nearly every Samhain dinner I've held. (Don't mess with a good thing, am I right?)

Dairy and animal products in general are quite important to the ancestral aspect of this celebration. Samhain was a time for our ancestors to cull their livestock for the harsh winter months, and there was often a surplus of meat and dairy products this time of year. If you do not have any dietary restrictions preventing it, I encourage you to be as authentic to that as possible.

You might host a dumb supper solo, with your immediate family, or with a group. For each of these scenarios, there are different ways to set the table. Typically, if I am alone for a dumb supper, I will sit at the foot of the table and make place settings in every other seat for specific people while creating the head of the table for my ancestral line at large. It is important to serve these plates and places before you come to yourself, being the last of the living line present at the table.

If you are hosting a dumb supper with immediate family, you can sit on one long side of the table, with your partner across from you on the other side. The head/foot of the table on your left-hand side should be made in tribute to your family, while your right-hand side will be for your partner. This way our family will always be on our left side, symbolically closest to our hearts and minds, while still being connected to the family at large.

In group settings, you follow the same principle as outlined above and have the place setting for your family directly to your left. This will mean that every other place setting is made available. Your family's settings should be adorned with items and articles they particularly liked, such as alcohol, food, candy, and photographs if you feel so inclined. This is to bring the spirit of your direct family to join in the congregation of celebration and commemoration. Your line is special; make sure they feel that way through your words and actions during this time.

HOMEGROWN CREAMY BUTTERNUT SQUASH SOUP

This soup is my starter for not only Samhain but pretty much all autumn meals in my house. I stumbled upon it after a great friend of mine lent me her mother's recipe. Every year I've tinkered with the ingredients as my diet changes, but overall it maintains the integrity of the original recipe. It is creamy and flavorful, and I somehow never get bored with it.

You will need a blender, because we will be blending our puree. This soup is especially good with a giant turkey meatball or matzo ball in it as well—but for Samhain it is best just plain. If you'd like to go a step further, I typically serve this in a carved-out pumpkin bowl. Experiment and see how you'd like to bring the flavors of the harvest to your supper table.

INGREDIENTS

- 2 medium butternut squash
- 2 tablespoons butter
- ½ cup shallots
- ½ cup onion
- 3 cloves garlic, minced
- 2 cups chicken or vegetable broth

- ¼ cup heavy whipping cream (or sub coconut milk)
- 1 teaspoon salt
- ½ teaspoon black pepper
- ¼ teaspoon dried rosemary
- ¼ teaspoon dried sage
- ¼ teaspoon allspice

Preheat oven to 400 degrees. Cover a large sheet pan with foil, cut the squash in half, and place them facedown on the pan. Bake in the oven until the squash is tender, about 1 hour 30 minutes. Set your oven on broil, flip the squash faceup, and broil the tops until lightly browned. Remove the squash from the oven and set aside to cool.

Melt butter in a stove pan over medium heat and sauté the shallots, onion, and garlic until they have reached a nice golden color, about five minutes. Remove from heat.

Once the squash has cooled, remove the seeds and scoop out the filling. You should have about 4½ cups of squash.

Add the shallots, onion, and garlic to a blender and blend until mostly smooth. Don't go crazy here—you'll be blending more throughout the process. Add the squash and blend again. Then add the broth and pulse to mix. (You may need to process the vegetables and broth in batches, depending on the size of your blender.)

Pour the blended squash into a big soup pot and stir in the cream. Heat over medium-high heat, stirring to mix. Add the salt, pepper, rosemary, sage, and allspice and stir.

Bring soup to a simmer and cook partially covered for 10 to 15 minutes.

Remove from heat and serve.

HARVEST RITUAL

If you have the space, the time, and the means, I highly recommend harvesting at least one item for your Samhain table, whether that's squash, garlic, herbs, or some other plant. This will allow the energy of the changing earth to come into your home and body in a way it wouldn't if you didn't take the effort to grow, nurture, and harvest a plant yourself. This is in no way mandatory, but it is fulfilling to eat what you've grown.

When you plant your seeds, sow the intention of connection. You will be nurturing and caring over these plants for weeks, which will in turn strengthen your connection to the spirit of the land, the spirit of your ancestry, and yourself. As you water them and tend to them, speak to them as though you are speaking to your loved ones. The messages will carry, and all of your conversations will be present on the Samhain table.

When you're ready to harvest, grab your garden shears and prepare an offering to the earth. This might mean making a mandala out of foraged items, picking up litter in the area, adding compost or other nutrient-rich soils, or bringing clean water. As the sun rises, go out to your plants and leave your offering. Before you cut the vine, thank the earth, sun, sky, rain, and spirit for providing this harvest.

Say "thank you" out loud, feeling the words radiate from your inner spirit out into nature. This is also a perfect time for reflection if you feel inclined to sit and meditate with these spirits and elements. The land that we live on and the spirits that reside on it alongside us are part of our immediate life. By sitting in their presence and acknowledging our gratitude, we strengthen our bonds to our spiritual surroundings.

10

YULE

[commonly december 21-january 1

winter solstice

second spoke on the dark side of the modern wheel of the year]

*If we had no winter, the spring would not be so pleasant: if we did not
sometimes taste of adversity, prosperity would not be so welcome.*

—Anne Bradstreet

In the beginning, there was darkness. Before the light came, before days and nights, solstices and equinoxes, there was only darkness. We are born out of darkness, and we return to darkness when we pass. This darkness is as much a part of us as we are of it; the presence of it is felt heavy through this section of the wheel of the year.

The first "dark harvest" in the wheel is Samhain, which is marked by a thinner veil, reverence for the dead, and harvesting plants and livestock. Yule, the second "dark harvest," is marked by these same features as some brighter ones as well. Yule, a Germanic origin festival (also known as winter solstice), is the second spoke on the dark side of the modern wheel of the year. It is a rich cultural folk holiday that has unique roots in nearly every culture. Thoughts of Yuletide invoke just as much light as darkness. From holly to garlands, wreaths, cookies, lights, and Yule logs, the pagan roots of this season are still an active part of secular and spiritual life.

Interestingly enough, Yule has not always been directly synonymous with the winter solstice and has instead been referred to as its own season. To be fair, when talking about Yule season, we should really start during the first week of December, when some of the other pagan and spiritual holidays start. These feast days lead us into the holiday season, so it would be fair to say that it starts there.

Nearly every culture has a holiday around the winter solstice, so this particular day is not specific to Celtic cultures or even owned by pagans. Nearly every spiritual practice can appreciate the importance of the darkest day of the year, the descent we took to get there, and the rebirth coming into the new year.

When looking at the origins of Yule, we find an interesting and slightly fuzzy history. The word *Yule* is English in origin, deriving from the Old English *geol*, which translates to *Christmastide*. This Old English word is thought to have been derived from the Old Norse *Jól*, which was a pagan winter solstice festival. The first time we get into the word *Yule* in its more modern forms occurred in the fifteenth century. What we can tell, however, looking at this rough etymology, is that modern Yule (which is now a largely English- and Anglican-influenced traditional holiday) has its roots in heathen Germanic and Norse practice and legend. Even with this interesting dichotomy between the Yule origin, many modern pagan practitioners follow the traditions of the Wiccan-influenced Yule, which has its origins in the English version of the festival.

Pagan Yule versus Heathen Jól

Before I diverge into the differences between Yule and Jól, I want to explain why I separated heathen and pagan for this section. The term *pagan* is an umbrella used to describe those beliefs and practices outside of the accepted Abrahamic traditions. Pagan beliefs include practices such as Wicca, druidism, and Hellenism. The word *pagan* is not necessarily used to describe Asian or indigenous faiths, as they often reject this term. The term *heathenry* specifically refers to Germanic paganism. This includes practices such as Asatru, Germanic paganism, Vanatru, Norse paganism, Saxon paganism, and the Northern Tradition. Heathenry has specific influences from the Germanic, Nordic, Scandinavian, and occasionally Anglo-Saxon peoples.

So what separates Yule and Jól? At first glance, the easiest thing to point out is the difference in timing. Both the pagan and heathen Yule occur in the month of December; however, the pagan Yule is the literal day of the winter solstice, whereas the heathen Yule begins around December 20 and runs until about December 31. If this feels reminiscent of the modern twelve days of Christmas, it's because it is.

Timing is not the only obvious difference. The days of the festivals can vary as well. The modern Yule from the wheel of the year is always on the winter solstice but can be observed the night before through the morning after. The older heathen Yule was observed around the end of December through the beginning of January. There was no set date to this observation, but it was typically observed around the time of the winter solstice.

One of the biggest key differences, however, is the acknowledgment of the dead at heathen Yuletide. Yule is the darkest part of the year, the time when the veil is thinnest between the living and the dead. To the outsider, this may sound similar to Samhain, but its very essence is so different in both tone and intention. The earth is dark, cold, and seemingly dead. It is the time for the Wild Hunt, but it is also a time to celebrate our friends, families, and other loved ones. It is a time of reflection and a time to rest from work.

In modern Yule celebrations, there is a strong focus on the rebirth of the sun. Yule is the tipping point from the darkest night of the year into the rebirth of the sun and all its blessings. This is not a somber time at all, nor does it celebrate or acknowledge the dead. This version of Yule is full of the promise of new life and the potential for joy. For Wiccans especially, Yule is one of two times in the year that the Holly King and the Oak King battle. At Yule the Oak King wins—but this will shift again come Litha, when the battle for light and dark renews.

Customs and Lore of Yule

Because no one culture, religion, or practice truly owns the spirit of Yule, we are blessed to have an abundance of festive myth. While some might say that certain practices are specific in origin, I believe that our nomadic European ancestors shared many of their beliefs with each other, giving us a widespread, almost uniform approach to the winter solstice season.

In the text *Religious Holidays and Calendars*, editor Karen Bellenir writes:

> *In many Pagan traditions, the concept of rebirth is expressed through the birth of a Divine Child. The celebration may include a vigil on the eve of Yule in anticipation of the birth. The child born at Yule is given different names in different legends. In Egyptian mythology the child is Horus; in Greco-Roman it is Apollo; in Norse it is Balder; in Phoenician it is Baal; and in Celtic it is Bel.*

I found it interesting that this textbook drew lines between the Christian concept of Christmas, the birth of the Divine Child Jesus Christ, and the births of many pagan gods.

From the Holly and Oak Kings to the witch goddess Frau Perchta and the Krampus, no festival season has invoked so much fear and joy in the same stroke. Arguably, though, no particular Yule myth has been as widespread as that of the Wild Hunt. The Wild Hunt was so infectious in folklore that it transcended Old Europe and was born again into today's modern world of Christmas lore.

Odin and the Wild Hunt

The Wild Hunt is one of the best known and most misunderstood Yule-time myths. The Wild Hunt is thought to be Germanic in origin but had several versions throughout Europe, each with its own unique spin.

In essence, the Wild Hunt was a processional horde of spirits, usually lead by Odin, that roamed through the night sky. Odin, on the back of his eight-legged steed, Sleipnir, would lead the horde, and as they passed, pounding hooves, raging winds, and howling dogs were present. In some versions of the myth, the horde would take up the souls of sinners; in others, they would pick up stray passersby and deposit them miles from where they were originally taken.

Through time, the Wild Hunt became less wild along the way. It is thought that the myth of Santa Claus is directly related to Odin. This is backed up by the evidence of Santa's eight reindeer paired against the eight-legged Sleipnir. Both Santa Claus and Odin gave gifts, and both Santa Claus and Odin had elves/dwarves that could make things for them!

Yuletide Traditions

Firelight and candlelight, candy canes and drifting snow . . . the season of Yuletide is here. Each culture has traditions that are observed around the Yule season, many of which have some of their roots in older, more sacred pagan or folk traditions. From Christmas trees to Yule logs, cookies, mistletoe, carols, and celebrations, there is no shortage of ways to ring in the end of the calendar year and the eve of the birth of the new one.

One of my personal favorite traditions is mistletoe. We all know about kissing under the mistletoe, but what is not so well-known is the fact that mistletoe has been used for thousands of years. The Greeks and Romans kept mistletoe for its medicinal purposes, using it to treat everything from menstrual cramps to epilepsy to poison.

The Celts associated mistletoe with romance, however. Mistletoe is one of the few things that can blossom during the frozen winter months—the druids saw this as a sign. During the first century, the Celtic druids believed that the blooming of the frozen mistletoe during the harsh winter months was a secret symbol of virility and fertility.

The Norse have folklore with mistletoe as well. According to mythology, Odin's son Baldr was prophesied to die. His mother, Frigg, went to all the plants and animals of the world securing an oath that they would not harm him. She overlooked and neglected to speak with the mistletoe, so Loki, a mischievous, shape-shifting god, made an arrow from mistletoe that was used to kill him.

Mistletoe went from being a sacred plant to a secular decoration sometime just before the eighteenth century, and it was incorporated into Christmas celebrations by pagan converts throughout history. Either way, mistletoe is a merry plant that reminds us to look for life amid the death of winter.

WITCH BALLS

Witch balls are glass tools that witches use to protect against evil spirits and sickness. During the Yuletide season, many stores are packed full of clear glass ornaments that are perfect for making your very own witch ball! There are tons of ways that they are made, but all witch balls have the same purpose. In folk traditions, they were used to protect the home and garden from evil spirits, or the evil eye.

In *Traditional Witchcraft*, Gemma Gary writes,

> These huge reflective mirrored glass "baubles" are often filled with protective herbs, and hung in a window. There are two modes of thought as to how these work. Some say they work to deflect or repel a curse or evil spirit that tries to enter the home, whilst others say that evil spirits are attracted by the bright reflective surface, and remain there until they are destroyed by the light of the morning sun, or are wiped out of the window with any dust that has settled on the globe.

Creating witch balls during Yule season is one of the most frugal (budget witches rejoice) do-it-yourself witchcraft projects you can possibly make! All you need are some clear glass ornaments, herbs, crystals if you want them, and any other small magickal tools you like.

Traditional witch balls are typically kept on a windowsill or altar or buried in a garden. Modern witch balls can be made for a variety of larger purposes such as communication, prosperity, or health and can be placed anywhere that you're wanting to charge the energy for a specific purpose. I've also seen witch balls left in a garden or on a front walkway to promote fertility of the land and protection of the house.

Crafting witch balls is a good exercise in working with your intuition. Set out all of your supplies on an altar or table before you, and channel the energy of the ball. If you are making a witch ball specifically for protection, I personally like to add a little cascarilla powder (see p. 191). Cascarilla powder is white, so it looks a bit like snow, which is nice for working in the Yule season. When all of the ingredients have been added to the ball, it is time to seal it.

There are two primary ways of sealing a witch ball: with wax or hot glue. For the wax method, melt some stamp wax and dip the tip of the ornament into the wax, covering all the metal parts until it touches the glass. Set aside to cool. Alternatively, you could use a hot glue gun to apply glue to the lid and rim of the witch ball, being careful not to get any glue on the inside. Put the cap over this lip and hold it in place until the glue sets. Add a ribbon or string to hang and your witch ball is complete.

II

IMBOLC

[january 31–february 2
saint brigid's day/candlemas
third spoke on the dark side of the modern wheel of the year]

If Candlemas day be sunny and bright, winter will have another flight;
if Candlemas day be cloudy with rain, winter is gone, and won't come again.

—proverb

Imbolc is the first fire festival in the dark half of the wheel. This is a festival where we begin to see the light of life returning to earth, as the sun begins noticeably waxing into spring. Imbolc is one of the four Celtic fire festivals (Samhain, Imbolc, Beltane, and Lughnasadh), which celebrates the return of light after the darkness of winter. This is also the time when the Goddess changes from the Crone to the Maiden.

Magickly, Imbolc is not only associated with the sun and fire but also with life, water, and divination. It is the midpoint between the winter solstice and the spring equinox. However, the festival is celebrated over multiple days and is not as time sensitive as Samhain. A festival of Celtic origin, Imbolc is originally thought to have been celebrated on February 1. However, it has moved to being observed on February 2, which merges it with the Candlemas celebration of the Catholic Church. Currently, the festival of Imbolc begins on what is known as February Eve, January 31, and continues through the end of February 2.

The etymology of Imbolc's origins actually is a little tricky to wrap our head's around even in its seeming simplicity. At its root, *Imbolc* is an Irish word thought to translate to "in the belly." Other sources believe that the word actually originates from an older medieval word, *oimelc*, which translates to "ewe's milk." Both translations do refer to ewes, as this is the time of year they are pregnant. Given that this is a fertility holiday, it should come as no surprise that the naming and origins reflects that. Interestingly enough, while we give credit to the Celtic people for the observation of Imbolc, it is thought that the earlier indigenous Irish not of Celtic origin celebrated this day first.

Saint Brigid's Day

In today's world, the Irish still celebrate Imbolc yearly, in a day known as the Feast of Saint Brigid, or Saint Brigid's Day. Retaining some of its pagan origins, Saint Brigid's Day became a Christian holiday in honor of the Irish patron saint Brigid of Kildare.

Brigid was born in County Kildare, Ireland, in 450. Her mother is thought to have been Brocca, a Pict slave who became a Christian after being baptized by Saint Patrick. Brigid's father was a Leinster chieftain, but this did not change her status as being born to a slave in slavery. She is attributed with converting several druid temples into Christian monasteries in Ireland. And she had many qualifying miracles throughout her lifetime that lifted her to sainthood, such as turning water into beer and curing two sisters who were mute by touching them with her blood after an injury. (If ever there was an Irish saint, it would be one who could turn water into beer.)

Most popularly, Imbolc is thought to be most closely associated with the goddess Brigid. This is shown in later years as the festival was converted by the Christian Church into what is now known as the Feast of Saint Brigid. The goddess Brigid was especially important to the Celtic people during the last phase of the winter season. Brigid was not only the goddess of childbirth and healers but also the goddess of the hearth and fire. During Imbolc, it is believed that her light will help to take the darkness out of winter and rejuvenate the earth with the warmth and light of the sun.

As the festival became popular throughout the British Isles, traditions such as creating the Brigid's cross and bride dolly's grew in popularity. The Brigid's cross, and Irish tradition, was a three to four-armed cross made out of woven rushes. These crosses were then hung over doors and windows for protection and to welcome the goddess Brigid into the hearth and home.

Many scholars debate if Saint Brigid was a real person or if she was a Christianization of the Celtic goddess Brigid. Some scholars believe that the overlap between the person and the goddess occurred after her death, making it easier to convert the pagan Irish population.

Frigga, Goddesses, and Gods

To many, Brigid absolutely embodies Imbolc. However, to many heathens, it is Frigga who dominates the season. Thinking in a secular way, the beginning of February brings with it love, lust (which can turn into children), and time spent inside to get out of the cold. Frigga was a goddess who wore many hats, but she was known best for being the wife of Odin, the Queen of Aesir, the goddess of fertility, marriage, hearth, and home. Essentially, all of the things that Frigga lords over are themes to Imbolc as well.

While the most popular deities for Imbolc celebrations are the goddesses Brigid and Frigga, this is a time of year for generally every god and goddess of love and fertility. Imbolc brings with it the first thoughts of the earth's fertility, the possibility of spring on the horizon. Much how popular secular culture celebrates love during this time of year, the gods are up to it, too.

For the specific holiday observance of Imbolc, aside from the generalized "Lord and Lady" and the goddess Brigid, there are not that many singled out gods or goddesses. There are other holidays that are closely associated with Imbolc that may even overlap in some way, shape, or form—but Imbolc is a purely Celtic origin holiday that is meant to focus on shaking off the cold and dark of winter and welcoming in the life-giving light and fertility of the sun.

Year of the Witch

Recovery and Renewal Festival

Imbolc is the perfect time to renew your devotion to your craft and to your gods. While we start the witch's year in autumn with Samhain, most of us did not begin our path on that day. And if you're like me, you probably didn't mark down on a calendar the first time you read a book on Wicca, paganism, or witchcraft and decided, "Hey, this might be for me." While I know I started sometime in 2001, I'd be hard-pressed to nail down an exact anniversary.

Putting this anniversary-type ritual around Imbolc happened pretty naturally for me. At the time I had started doing this, I was living in northwest Montana. The winter was usually long and harsh, and it allowed a lot of time to reflect on myself, my practices, and the future. During this time of the year, most places in the northern hemisphere are on the cusp of spring. Light is returning after months of cold darkness! The earth is once again pregnant with the magick and possibility of new life. This is a special time when we can embody this light and take a moment to appreciate it within ourselves and our craft. This little ritual is truly for everyone, because regardless of whether you have been formally initiated into a coven or you have a solitary practice, there was once a day when you made a personal commitment to yourself to continue following your path.

Thinking back to when I first started doing this ritual in a solitary (and occasionally group) way, I would be lying if I said I had it all figured out. The most important thing to remember while doing this is your commitment to yourself. The commitment we made as pagans and witches before we found a god or goddess is the most important commitment we can keep. Additionally, if things don't feel right as written, change them to fit you! Reading how others initiate their rituals lays the framework for supporting how we build our own. If something I've written doesn't speak to you, replace it with something that does!

There comes a point, however, when beginning witches realize they either no longer want to or can't remain as a solitary island and continue growing spiritually. At some point, we almost all branch out at least a little. If you have a desire to do more group-oriented spellwork and rituals, finding a coven might be the next phase of your journey! I have found that the best way to meet more witches is to go to places witches gather—your local metaphysical or witch shop, a crystal store, a drum circle or concert. When you get there, branch out! Talk to people, and really try to engage. Some stores maintain a list of events that they or others host in the store. By attending these events and networking, you will soon find your way to creating lasting and meaningful witch relationships.

SELF-INITIATION AND RENEWAL RITUAL

As the earth is welcoming in the light of life, we'll take our cues from nature and welcome that same energy into our lives and homes. A few days before Imbolc, you'll want to build an altar for this ceremony, either indoors at an east-facing window or outdoors. Gather the following items:

- 2 red candles
- 2 orange candles
- 2 white candles
- A cauldron
- Salt
- Rubbing alcohol
- Fresh flowers
- Your favorite food or drink

- Notebook and pen
- A set of unscented tealight candles

Set the candles in a semicircle. In the center of the candle arc, arrange your cauldron, salt, and alcohol. Then arrange your flowers, food or drink offering, and pen in a way that's pleasing to you. The tealight candles don't need to be placed on your altar, but could be stored nearby. They'll be used during the ritual.

I like to take the first day of Imbolc in reverence to my gods, the second day in remembrance of my path, and the third day in celebration. So traditionally, this ritual should be performed on February 1, either as the sun is rising or while it is still up in the sky.

Light one tealight candle in each room of your house, not counting the hallways. Starting at the far east room in your house, light a candle anywhere that is safe to light. Repeat this process, going clockwise through your home, welcoming in and literally bringing in the light of the sun and its blessings.

When the clock has come full circle, it is time to begin to work at the altar. This is not a petitioning ritual, or a ritual involving gods or ancestors, but if you feel intuitively called to welcome them into this space with you, then call out to them. After all, you are choosing to share your spiritual life with them.

Light the candles in the semicirlce on the altar from left to right as you repeat this phrase:

From darkness to light,
And from light to night,
Renew and restore,
With these, I do pour.

Once all the candles are lit, prep the eternal fire that is in all of our hearts. Pour an inch of salt into your cauldron. Pour the rubbing alcohol on top just until the salt is saturated. Set aside. When you are ready, take one of the candles and carefully touch the flame to the salt in your cauldron. Doing this will ignite the alcohol and create a small fire.

As the fire burns, visualize your intention and dedication to your craft. What drew you to this path? What keeps you there? How can you continue to grow throughout the coming year?

Take out your notebook and pen and write down affirming "I will" statements. As each year progresses, you will be able to look back at the prior years' "I wills" and see how many you were able to accomplish. (Last year I wrote, "I will write a book.")

When you have finished writing, look into the fire and focus your energy. Read each of your "I will" statements aloud three times. The first time, you read it for yourself. The second time, you read it for your shadow self (see p. 148). The third and final time, you read it for your spirit. Allow the words to slowly sink into each level of consciousness, manifesting the will and desire you have to enact change.

As you draw the ritual to a close, focus your attention on the food or drink that you brought as an offering. You are the one you're offering to. Partake in the indulgence, knowing that by receiving an offering yourself, you are sealing a pact to take the next year head-on and tackle your goals.

12

OSTARA

[march 21/22

spring equinox

fourth spoke on the dark side of the modern wheel of the year]

You can cut all the flowers but you cannot keep spring from coming.

—Pablo Neruda

L ight and dark meet in the middle twice a year. Ostara is the spring
equinox, which means that the length of night and day are equal.
Equinox descends from *aequus*, the Latin word for "equal," and *nox*, the
Latin word for "night."

Thought to be Roman in origin, Ostara predates Wicca and Chris-
tianity. Ostara is thought to have been established by Caesar to mark
the beginning of the tropical year. And contrary to popular belief, while
Easter does share a lot of similarities with Ostara, they are not the same
thing. Easter is the first Sunday after the first full moon following the
spring equinox. That is why Easter can be celebrated in late March or
early April. In general, the religious celebration of Easter has nothing to
do with the secular traditions of eggs, rabbits, and candy that are popular with the springtime holiday today.

There is variance of the Ostara holiday found all throughout the
world. The spring equinox symbolizes rebirth, revival, and resurrection,
as it is the last festival in the dark half of the wheel. The warming temperatures also lead to increased fertility, and it is a great time to begin
planting the seeds of love magick. To look around outside, you would
begin to notice that the earth is fertile, pregnant with the possibility of
life just about to spring forth from the ground. Some Wicca traditions
hold that the Goddess and the God are married at Ostara.

Throughout European history, and much of world history even, it
was commonplace to give a couple livestock to encourage and promote
fertility in their union.

Gods and Goddesses of Ostara

Spring brings with it a wealth of gods and goddesses coming out of winter and rejuvenating the earth with life! There are so many worshipped across all cultures, but here are some of the most popular:

Eostre: Ostara is named after the Anglo-Saxon goddess of spring, Seostara or Eostre. Even with a modern holiday being named after her, not much is actually known about the goddess Eostre.

Pan: Ostara brings with it the return of the Horned God in a new form, Pan. Pan is a god of nature and the wild. He brings in the coming spring with his songs, waking up the slumbering animals through the wilderness.

Triple goddess: Looking at the gods and goddesses of Ostara, we also tend to see various goddess aspects of the great triple goddess as she resumes her Maiden form. This is true of any triple goddess, and not delegated to a particular one.

Persephone (Kore): In Greek mythology, Persephone is also linked to Eostre, as the flowers and birds are beginning to return from their winter hiatus. We can find Demeter, who is caring for her daughter Persephone, after her time spent in the underworld.

Spring Cleaning

It is no coincidence that we have a tradition of spring cleaning. As the last spoke on the dark half of the year, Ostara is just on the cusp of a new season of life in nature. Not only have our physical spaces gotten dusty, sometimes our mental spaces have too. Spring, and Ostara in particular, is where we tend to ourselves and restore the balance in our physical and spiritual spaces.

Most of us know Marie Kondo's theory for decluttering and cleaning our lives. This is a physical practice that deeply affects our spiritual well-being. Cleaning, tidying up, and decluttering not only allow us to breathe, but they allow us to decide what we devote energy to daily. We have the choice to maintain lots of things or fewer things. When we have lots of things in our lives, the physical clutter is a direct reflection of internal clutter that we may have.

I see this as kindly as I can, as I am a clutterer myself, and I feel fairly confident in saying that if you clutter your space, there is some aspect of either your spiritual or mental life that is cluttered as well. It's one of those basic concepts that you can find in almost any self-help book, but it's really true. Do we control our belongings, or do our belongings control us?

If you think things have gotten out of hand, don't worry. You can follow the basic process of decluttering that follows. And remember, you're not decluttering just to declutter; your decluttering to allow spiritual growth and energy to flow through your space.

SPRING CLEANING AND DECLUTTERING RITUAL

I will be the first person to admit that I am cluttered. I have tried nearly every "hack" to get organized yet still find myself amid a sea of chaos in my daily life. Sound familiar? If so, this one is for you.

You will need:

- **White seven-day jar candle**
- **Large garbage bags**

- **Broom**
- **Mop**
- **Florida water (see p. 193)**
- **Salt**
- **A few free hours**

Begin by lighting the candle and placing it on your working altar. Ask your higher powers to lend you peace as you begin this task. Leave the candle burning as much as possible, preferably letting it burn straight through.

Take a few moments to center yourself in meditation. Reflect on what area in your physical world brings you the most stress. When you feel grounded, grab those trash bags and head to that area.

Put everything (except furniture and items that are 100 percent necessary for daily function) into the bags and place them in a closet or closed room.

Grab your broom and sweep in a clockwise motion, moving the dirt out of the room and out the front door.

Next, prepare your mop by placing a pinch of salt and a generous amount of cleansing herbs (see p. 45) or Florida water into a bucket of cold water. Mop the floor in a counterclockwise motion. Allow your floors to dry completely before using them again.

Do not return to the bags of stuff until the seven-day candle has burned all the way down (or wait seven days before going back to the bags). This will allow you the clarity and space to declutter and start fresh.

Eggs at Easter

Dyeing Easter eggs is a popular secular tradition we've probably all partaken in at some point in our lives. In the Middle Ages, Europeans began decorating eggs as a treat following Easter Sunday mass. These eggs were eaten to break the fast from Lent, and this is still something that occurs in parts of Europe today. The original intent behind dyeing eggs was to encourage the sun to get brighter, which is why so many Easter eggs incorporate the color yellow. Eggs are the ultimate symbol of fertility and potential, a time when we are finally coming out of the darkness of winter and the light of spring is just around the corner.

Regardless of its actual origin, what we do know is that decorating eggs is a central activity in today's modern Easter traditions. So why not have a little bit of fun with it?

OSTARA EGGS

There are tons of ways to dye eggs, but the best way to foster that energy of fertility is to use natural elements instead of boxed dyes. There are tons of plants that can provide beautifully colored eggs if you're willing to give it a shot.

When selecting materials for naturally dyed eggs, it's best to use fresh or frozen produce. Canned vegetables and fruits typically lose their color and aren't very pleasing. Here are a few ingredients I have found over the years to dye eggs natural colors. Some work better than others, but I have successfully (or unintentionally) managed all of these colors using these ingredients:

- Red: lots of yellow onion skins; beets; chokecherries; raspberries
- Pink: beets, cranberries, cherries

- Orange: yellow onion skins, carrots
- Yellow: saffron, cumin, turmeric, chamomile tea
- Green: spinach
- Blue: blueberries, red cabbage, hyacinth, butterfly pea flowers or tea
- Purple: wine

When you're using natural dyes, it's easiest to hard-boil your eggs and your dye materials at the same time. Boil eggs as you usually would and set them aside. In a large mason jar or bowl, prepare your boiled dyes. When you have placed the dye in whatever container you will use for your eggs, place the eggs in and let them sit for a few hours. Adding a little bit of vinegar to the water will help enhance the color. Remove them from the liquid, and allow them to dry.

Alternatively, you can soak hard-boiled eggs in room-temperature dye for longer.

(Note: Red eggs need to be boiled with copious amounts of yellow onion and vinegar, and will take longer.)

When you dye eggs with natural products, they aren't glossy like how boxed dyes make them. However, you're probably not done with your eggs yet, and will use paint or markers to add designs. Once you've finished designing your eggs, coat them with a little bit of vegetable oil to give them a nice sheen.

A Time to Recommit to Our Goals

Ostara is this unique time of year when we are just coming out of the dormant stages of winter but are not quite able to jump into the active stages of spring and summer. For whatever reason, I am really averse to the light that filters through in April and find that the earth is overall too bright and buzzy and happy. Maybe I just wish that it were still autumn, or perhaps I am just going through a little bout of seasonal depression. Either way, I find that during this time I often struggle with maintaining motivation to work toward the goals I set in the Imbolc period—this is the time of year I am most inclined to be lazy.

So I created a spell against laziness for just this type of problem. Performing a series of steps is actually very similar to forming a new habit. We can't objectively target and work on our problems unless we are able to identify them. By giving ourselves the ability to objectively look at what is working and what is not working, we empower ourselves to maintain power over our reality.

DUST-BANISHING RITUAL
(OR: A RITUAL TO FORM A NEW HABIT)

This ritual is perfect for whenever you feel as though you've sort of lost track of your goals or your momentum to accomplish the things you want to get done. It helps you hit the reset button and come back to your focused self with fresh eyes and energy, a kind of antidote to that post–New Year's resolution slump.

You'll need to assemble a few basic supplies to start:

- **A talisman that you will wear every day**
- **A notebook and pen**
- **A seven-day candle**

A talisman is a piece of jewelry or other trinket that is used in spellwork for protection and to bring good fortune or wealth. This doesn't have to be some large sign of paganism if you are either closeted or work a professional day job. Personally, I like to wear Alex and Ani charm bracelets. They are inconspicuous enough to wear in daily life without question, affordable, and have tons of different varieties for whatever the mood of my spell is.

To set the tone, light your seven-day candle and invoke the elements, spirits, gods/goddesses, or guides that you would like to walk with you on your path to activity. Do not call on someone unless you want to work with them continually for the next few weeks.

Grab your notebook and pen, sit back, and jot down what your day looks like. Start from the time you wake up to the time you lay down—all of the things you usually do and how you do them.

Look objectively at the list and write down some of the areas you want to work on. Which one of these is most manageable right now? Circle one item on the list of changes that you'd like to make. (Note: This shouldn't be the biggest problem on the list, because that problem probably isn't manageable right now.)

Write out the sequence of events in which this problem or behavior occurs.

Then write out the sequence of events as you want them to happen, changing the process.

Whatever your pattern is, write it down on a new sheet of paper. As a bonus, drawing a sigil to charge your new daily ritual can help you maintain motivation during the first few days. Sigils are small symbols made by a witch or occultist to embody a particular spell or manifestation.

When you've figured our your new pattern (and sigil), leave the paper, along with your talisman, to charge with the seven-day candle. Leave the candle burning and come back to it each day for the duration of the burn.

With each day that passes, assess what is working about your new pattern and what isn't.

The reason we are leaving the talisman with the burning candle is because creating a new ritual to replace a faulty one rarely works the first time around. Allow yourself a few minutes throughout each day that the candle is burning to come back and be honest about your progress and what might need correcting.

At the end of the seventh day (or however long it takes your jar candle to burn), pick up the talisman and prepare to "banish the dust." Grab some good old-fashioned cleaning supplies and literally dust off all the surfaces in your house, setting your intention to continue with your new patterns and rituals daily.

13

BELTANE

[april 30/may 1 (halfway between spring equinox and summer solstice)

may day

first spoke on the light side of the modern wheel of the year]

There are lots of ways to interpret the meaning of the word fertility. Actually, creativity, being a broader term, might be a better word to use. We do like to honor our past, though, so most of us say fertility even if we haven't planted any crops and even if we don't hope to find ourselves in the family way.

—Ashleen O'Gaea, *Celebrating the Seasons of Life: Beltane to Mabon*

B eltane is a fire festival and starts the light half of the wheel of the year. The four dark holidays—Samhain, Yule, Imbolc, and Ostara—have passed, and this is the time to welcome in the light of the sun and new life. Like many festivals on the light side of the year, Beltane is primarily a fertility festival.

Maypoles, Puritans, and Perseverance

A shining example of Beltane fertility, maypoles represent new vegetation and new growth—and the celebration around them reflects our joy in the planet's return, among many other things. Historians believe that the practice of dancing around the maypole dates back to prehistoric times. Rock carvings have been found in Scandinavia that are believed to depict the sacred marriage between the human representatives of the God and the Goddess in the spring to fertilize the land and encourage vegetation and growth.

According to Michael Howard, author of *The Sacred Ring: Pagan Origins of British Folk Festivals and Customs*, some of the earliest European references to the maypole come from the fourteenth century, in the works of an unknown poetic bard. These tales refer to the raising of birch maypoles. The raising of the maypole was linked with Morris dancing, a form of English folk dancing where garlands were hung with silver spoons, watches, tankards, and symbols of the sun, stars, and moon. If this sounds familiar, it's because similar themes and scenes are found throughout the wands suit in the Rider-Waite-Smith tarot deck.

In the sixteenth century, a London vicar ordered the city maypole to be cut down because it was seen as a symbol of idol worship. Then England was split between the monarchy and republicanism, and maypoles were outlawed by the Puritan leader Oliver Cromwell. This was a time when puritanism was popular, so the whole concept of the maypole was considered to be a heathen abomination. While in power, Cromwell had outlawed maypoles to such an extreme that he would send soldiers out to find people continuing the folk tradition in private. The people, being smarter than the Puritan ruler at the time would hide their maypoles under the eaves of their houses, where the soldiers were unable to find them.

After Cromwell's reign, the monarchy was reinstated and so was the maypole. In fact, Charles II rode past a maypole on the way to his coronation, as it was a focal point of the celebrations for the people of London and Westminster.

Historically, some people used whole trees and decorated them much like we do Christmas trees. Others used actual poles, typically made of birch or ash, both of these having traditional spiritual significance. The birch is a sacred tree to the Goddess and represents fertility and new beginnings, and the World Tree in Norse mythology was supposedly an ash.

Beltane Bonfires

Beltane is one of the four Gaelic fire festivals and the sabbat that is most synonymous with bonfires. In *Religious Holidays and Calendars*, editor Karen Bellenir writes, "Depending on the preferences of the people conducting the ceremony, the Beltane fire may be kindled on Walpurgis Night (May Eve) or on Beltane (May 1). By tradition, the Beltane fire contains bundles of nine different types of wood chosen for their symbolism and associated attributes." Although exactly which woods are used is unclear (it appears they change in each source, probably due to regional variation), Pauline and Dan Campanelli, in their book *Wheel of the Year*, compiled a list of woods that should be harvested in March to allow for proper drying in time for Beltane:

Apple

Birch

Fire

Grapevine

Hawthorn

Hazel

Oak

Rowan

Willow

These sacred Beltane fires have been used historically for ritual, community, and luck. In *The Stations of the Sun*, Ronald Hutton explains,

> *The earliest reference to it [Beltane] is probably in Sanas Chormaic, an early medieval Irish glossary. . . . Under the entry "Beltane," both surviving texts have "'lucky fire,' i.e. two fires which Druids used to make with great incantations, and they used to bring the cattle against the diseases of each year to those fires." In the margin of one is the additional jotting "they used to drive the cattle between them."*

Hutton continues,

> The flames on the eve or the day were also used to bless and protect
> humans, who leaped them. The best description of this custom in
> country districts was furnished in 1852 by Sir William Wilde:
>
> > . . . If a man was about to perform a long journey, he
> > leaped backwards and forwards three times through the fire, to
> > give him success in his undertaking. If about to wed he did it
> > to purify himself for the marriage state. If going to undertake
> > some hazardous enterprise, he passed through the fire to render
> > himself invulnerable. As the fire sunk low, the girls tripped
> > across it to procure good husbands; women great with child
> > might be seen stepping through it to ensure a happy delivery,
> > and children were also carried across the smouldering ashes.
> > At the end the embers were thrown among the sprouting crops
> > to protect them, while each household carried some back to
> > kindle a new fire in its hearth (Sir William R. Wilde, Irish
> > Popular Superstitions [Dublin, 1852], 39–40, 47–49).

In its more modern form, Beltane fires and festivals are a reason
to celebrate the joy of living and being alive. In *Celebrating the Seasons of
Life: Beltane to Mabon*, Ashleen O'Gaea reminds us that one of the attributes of solar energy is the capacity to fertilize and stimulate growth.
And that the great bonfires at the beginning of summer represent the
creative heat and the light in the warmth of fertility of all kinds, from
the fires we feel in our loins to forged fires and the fires of poetic
inspiration.

RELEASE CEREMONY

Fires are cathartic, a source of life and a source of relief. In my high school years, I attended a boarding school in very rural Montana. Once a year, the whole student body would attend what was called a "burn ceremony." This tended to be in the late spring to early summer, somewhere between May and July. During this ceremony, students would bring letters they had written, photos, and items that held particularly painful or toxic memories. One by one, each person would stand up and explain what they were burning, why they were burning it, and what they hoped the outcome would be.

At the time, I was dealing with the grief of losing my father. I had written a letter to him, so when it was my turn to stand up, I said something along the lines of, "I wrote this letter to my dad to tell him how I feel about his death. I will not let this control me anymore." It was in this moment that I reclaimed my narrative on who I was and what I was going to do.

I was born an only child to an isolated family. I lost both of my parents between the ages of ten and thirteen very suddenly. From there, I was shipped to boarding school, out of sight and out of mind for family members who did not want to (or have the ability to) take me in. I held this anger, hurt, and bitterness for years. I let it consume me. I took a very pessimistic worldview and became extremely distrustful of others.

Leading up to this burn ceremony, I knew it was something I wanted to let go. I didn't know what that was going to look like or how it was going to work out in the long run, but I knew that I couldn't allow myself to keep living in the role of a victim. I decided to hatch this plan to identify, target, and constructively remove learned behaviors and personality traits.

Year of the Witch

You will need:

- A large fire (preferably in a pit or bonfire)
- A pen
- A paper

Sitting down, the first part of this is to plan. Center yourself in your body and turn inward. Think about any part of your personality that no longer serves you. It's a good practice to begin with something that is attainable to change, versus a habit that is lifelong. Good places to start might look like, "I put myself down in front of others" or "I allow people to mistreat me." Whatever that trait is, write it at the top of the page. If you're struggling to find a trait, phone a friend. (Humans aren't an island; sometimes the best way to find out that you have a tail is by someone telling you!)

Next, write a letter to yourself as though you are giving advice to your best friend. How would you talk to them? How would you guide them? If the friend is constantly putting themselves down, how would you hold space for their pain while opening the door to healing?

When the letter is written, it is time to light the flame. I think this is better as a group exercise, because there is something healing about letting yourself be vulnerable with someone or a group of people you trust. This allows them to support you and hold you accountable and allows you to do the same for them.

Whether you are alone or in a group, walk around the fire in a circle, going counterclockwise as you read your letter aloud. As you finish, speak the words, "This no longer has control over me. Like a phoenix, I will rise," as you throw your letter into the fire. If you are in a group, allow others to do the same process. Sit in silence and meditate on what just happened.

Lastly, when you return back to your house, journal about your experience and how you felt about it. Check in with this journal entry once a week for a month. How far have you come from releasing that narrative?

Bel

The etymology of the word *Beltane*, like many of these holidays, is shrouded in a dose of healthy mystery. It is believed to be of Scottish Gaelic origins, coming from the word *Bealltainn*, which roughly translates to "May 1." This word comes from the root *bhel*, which means "to shine, flash, or burn," with the Old Irish word *ten*, which translates to "fire." Others have suggested that the root of this word can be traced back to the proto-Celtic god Balor.

The god Bel, or Balor, was known as "the bright one," as the Celtic prefix *bel-* is roughly translated to "bright" or "fortunate." Bel is thought by some to have been a sun god, while other historians argue that earlier Celtic clans saw the sun as a feminine aspect and do not attribute him to the sun at all. It is said that Lugh blinded Balor and replaced him as the alpha solar god.

During this time of year we remember the Goddess in her fire aspects as well, typically as Brigid, a triple fire goddess. As with all fire celebrations, Brigid does play a central role for many people during this time of year. What is interesting about Brigid is that there are a lot of stories of her union with the sun god at this season.

Creating a Spiritual Retreat

Beltane brings with it the beginning of light and the return of longer days. The harsh reality of winter is over, and our food supplies are generally safe. Overall, Beltane feels very secure, and it's no wonder, since it's smack in the middle of Taurus season. However, no matter how secure you may feel now, there will be times in the future when you don't feel this way. Creating a special place to spiritually retreat to will allow you to unwind from the physical and mental burdens of life.

It's just a fact of life that if you work in any sort of way throughout your day, you will encounter situations and people that are beyond your control. Not everyone can handle dealing with this power loss or struggle and feel crushed under the weight of that particular brand of pressure. The good news is, what you decide to do with your stress is ultimately what's going to change your situation. The tried-and-true advice of "we cannot change the wind, but we can adjust the sails" has its place in a witch's spiritual life.

I first decided to make a spiritual retreat about five years ago, while I was seeing a therapist to work through some trauma I had experienced as a young woman. We worked on a technique of building a place in my mind where I could retreat to when life got too overwhelming, and this method is applicable to a wide variety of situations and I believe it would help anyone. Being able to turn off the world when you choose to is a big accomplishment, and with practice it is something we all can achieve.

MINDFUL MEDITATION

I've found that the best way to handle stress is through intentional, mindful meditation. The best time for this practice is in the morning before work or school, but you can also do it at the end of your day if you find that you are too pressed for time in the morning. I like to give myself about thirty minutes to be fully immersed.

To begin, put on some instrumental music that isn't distracting but is pleasant to listen to. Put a blanket down on the floor and lay flat on your back.

Close your eyes, and slowly reach your hands up above your head, feeling your back muscles stretch slightly.

Return your arms to your sides and flex your feet forward until you feel a slight stretch in your legs. After a few seconds return your feet to a normal position.

Breathing deeply, feel your chest rise and fall for five counts.

Imagine you are standing at the top of a spiral staircase in your mind's eye. As you descend the stairs, take long, even breaths, making sure to release each breath for as long as you let it in.

When your foot touches the first step, a light forms above your head. On the second step, the light starts moving over your head and shoulders. On the third step, the light continues moving downward and warming you from the inside out.

Now you take a fourth step, nearly encompassed in this warm, purifying light. As you take the fifth and final step, you are light, safe, warm, pure. Once you have reached this final step, you will see a door in front of you. Walk to it and open it up. Step inside and see a place of peace and tranquility.

Sit in this space and feel the ground. Touch it with your fingertips, lay in it, and feel the surrounding air. Allow the light from earlier to surround you and fill you with peace. This is your sacred space. You can come back here whenever you desire by opening the door.

When you are relaxed and ready to leave, return to the door. Ascend the steps back to your body.

Feel the floor under you, your hands by your side. Raise your arms up over your head and stretch life back into them. When you are ready, open your eyes.

I do go to this sacred space a lot during my day when I need a break from my fast-paced life. I go to a place of rolling hills and trees, with cool air and a nice breeze. Wherever you go will be perfect for you as well.

This guided meditation can be done without any special materials. You can, however, call upon your intuition to create a full ritual with candles, an altar, and other props.

14

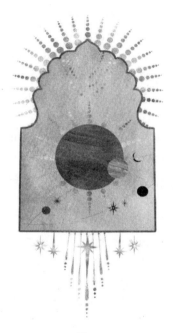

LITHA

[june 21

midsummer, summer solstice

second spoke on the light side of the modern wheel of the year]

The sun does not shine for a few trees and flowers, but for the wide world's joy.

—Henry Ward Beecher

Litha, also known as Midsummer, is the celebration of the summer solstice. It typically occurs on June 21, opposite of the winter solstice. A fire festival, we see the gods in their full glory after the death, sleep, and rebirth that occurred during fall, winter, and spring. Litha is the longest day of the year in the northern hemisphere, when the sun is as far north as it is ever going to get.

The summer solstice was widely celebrated throughout northern and western Europe and is believed to have been a big feature in the Celtic communities throughout Britain, Wales, Scotland, and Ireland. Like many folk holidays, the Church did try to take over the solstice and moved most of the festival to June 24, which they renamed Saint John's Day.

Being in the light half of the wheel, Midsummer has fire festival associations, same as Beltane, and large bonfires are lit to symbolize the sun, sensuality, life, and fertility. Festivals that take place during this time of year tend to have similar themes and are differentiated by specific celestial events and minor nuances. This means many of the same themes that were present through Beltane are going to be around for Litha and the rest of the summer sabbats.

Where death is a large feature through the dark half of the year, life is a big, if not the biggest, feature through the light half. What brings light more than love, laughter, and fertility? They are vibrant and alive at this time; it can be seen throughout nature and flowers especially.

Midsummer has been celebrated throughout the world. Egyptians designed the Great Pyramids in such a way that when viewed from the Sphynx, the sun will set precisely between two of the pyramids during the summer solstice. On the coast of Peru, archaeologists discovered the ancient Chankillo observatory complex with buildings that aligned with the sun during the solstices. Stonehenge, which is thought to be over five thousand years old, is aligned with both the summer and the winter solstice. To this day there are still large festivals held at the henge every solstice and equinox.

The etymology of Litha is actually really interesting, because it was entirely created in the mid-twentieth century. That's not to say that this word wasn't around before then, but it wasn't used as it is today to describe the Midsummer festival. When Wicca was in its early creation phase, and the wheel was just being developed, the creators drew from Celtic and druidic influences. It is believed that Litha is derived from an eighth-century article called "The Reckoning of Time." The name Litha was the last name for both June and July in ancient times. While this is somewhat accurate, *Notes and Queries: A medium of intercommunication for literary men, general readers, etc.* (the seventh volume in the series, written in 1889) gives us a better understanding on the topic.

In this book there are many notes on the Anglo-Saxon names of the month. It tells us that June and July are described as numbered months of the year. Month six is labeled as *Se āerra Litha*, which is translated to "the former Litha." Month seven is listed as *Se æftera Litha*, which is translated to "the latter Litha." In this dictionary, it states that "the name Litha is merely the definite form of Līthe, meaning mild, so that June and July are the mild, or warm months."

The Oak King and the Holly King

At Litha, the Oak King is at his peak, but he is forced to look at the challenges that winter will bring. It is believed that the Oak King, who rules the sun and summer, is the Goddess's consort. This means that the Oak King is her partner in love, fertility, and abundance. When we talk about the garden goddess in this aspect, in a generalized way, we are really talking about embodiments for the season.

Because this is a summer solstice festival, any solar god can be worshipped. This means not only Celtic sun gods, but the sun gods in every tradition. While not necessarily worshipped by northwestern Europeans, there are a number of Egyptian sun gods and goddesses that can be acknowledged during this time. For starters, the cat goddess Bastet is closely associated with the sun and is one of the daughters of Ra. We also have Horus, god of the sky. His right eye was the sun and his left one was the moon. This would put him at both the winter and the summer solstice. There's also Nefertem, god of healing and beauty, who represents the first sunlight.

In Nordic traditions, we have the sun goddess Sol, who traveled across the heavens every day in a chariot drawn by horses with manes of fire.

Then there's Kupala, Slavic water goddess of trees, herbs, sorcery, and flowers. June typically start some of the rainiest seasons in most climates, so it's quite fitting to have a water goddess represented in this festival season.

Shadow Self and Shadow Work

Shadow work is intensely personal, and how you decide to connect with your shadow self is your business. Shadow work is the work we undertake to meet our most authentic self. The longer we avoid our shadow work, the longer our pain festers, leaving our true selves sick and injured. This is the importance of shadow work: to objectively look at ourselves without the goal to change and instead accept what is on the other end. The practice of shadow work teaches us that we can't run away from ourselves, and why would we want to?

FLORAL SHADOW BONFIRE

Floral shadow work is one of the most intimate ways of approaching our shadow selves. Working with florals invokes the most tender, delicate aspects of our spirit that we tend to hide out of fear. Some of us never invoke the tender parts of our personality and may have even forgotten how to access them. The process is not an overnight journey, and you may never find that you are comfortable being tender. The courage to be vulnerable is a strength that not everyone has. Regardless, every person can work through this ritual and begin the task of accessing and healing their bruised and tender bits. The journey to self-love is difficult, but it is some of the most important work you will ever do.

Perform this ritual on a Sunday night, if you can. I have found that it is best to start your week lighter than you left it. If you feel called to do this on another day, that's absolutely fine too. There are no hard-and-fast rules; this is just another tool for self-care.

You can modify this ritual to your needs. If you live in a climate where you are unable to have a fire, feel free to substitute a candle, cauldron, or electric light. Or you could use another geographical feature and invoke a completely different element: old-growth forests, mountains, and the beach are great alternatives for anyone who doesn't feel comfortable using fire.

Before you start, you will need to have identified the traits of your personality that no longer serve you. Have these in a list or in your brain.

You will also need to consider any items that carry emotional baggage and weigh you down. This is absolutely vital to the success of creating vulnerable freedom within the boundaries and energy of the Litha season. Items that carry baggage might be things such as pictures of ex-partners, or a book, CD, or DVD that brings up bad memories. Don't torture yourself by holding on to physical stuff that hurts your shadow. Allow yourself to release that attachment to the pain and what it symbolized. You are no longer there and can let go.

You will need:

- Bonfire (candle, cauldron, or electric light if indoors)
- Sharpie
- Paper (bay leaves if indoors)
- Flowers
- Any items that carry emotional baggage and weigh you down
- Water or something to put out a fire

To start, light your fire. If you are in a safe place to be unrobed, the fewer clothes, the better.

Walk around the fire in a circle, making sure that it is lit from all angles. As the sparks become a flame, call on your higher power to join you in this circle of fire.

One by one, write each undesirable personality trait you are giving back to the universe on a piece of paper. When you are ready, take each piece and repeat the following:

> I release this energy to you, Higher Power, with love and grace.
> I ask that you relieve me of the burden I place upon myself.
> I call myself to action in relieving this burden as well.
> As it has been, it will not continue to be.
> Guide me now, Higher Power, through the garden of my mind.
> Walk with me as I navigate the shores of my spirit.
> Lay with me in the fields of my youth.
> For you have come before me, and you will be here after me as well.
> My trust, I place in you.
> So be it.

Throw the paper into the fire. Repeat this process until you no longer have any papers left.

Next, arrange the flowers you have brought with you in your hair. As you do, visualize your most tender parts being front and center. Allow the soft parts to lead the way as you close the ritual.

BASIC FLOWER CORRESPONDENCES

Following are a few flowers that could be used during this ritual:

African daisy: magick, intuition, psychic ability, protection
Bleeding heart: attract love, heal pain and depression, beauty, glamour
Bougainvillea: beauty, passion
Carnation: love, friendship
Chamomile: serenity, positivity, health and healing
Clover: prosperity, faery communication, protection
Daisy: friendship, health
Dandelion: divination, fertility, resilience
Foxglove: emotional healing, protection, faery connection
Heather: ancestral connection, heal trauma, protection, shadow work, past lives
Hibiscus: friendship, passion, lust and romance, intelligence
Honeysuckle: releasing sexual blocks, lust, intuition
Jasmine: sexuality, sensuality, joy
Lavender: clarity, cleansing, balance, relaxation
Lily: divine assistance, cleansing, legal success
Marigold: health and healing, reincarnation, vitality
Peony: cleansing, spiritual protection
Rose: abundance, friendship, love, secrecy, beauty
Snapdragon: hex and hex reversal, protection
Sunflower: happiness, power, strength, vitality

15

LUGHNASADH
FREY FEST, LAMMAS

[august 1
beginning of the harvest season
third spoke on the light side of the modern wheel of the year]

There are people in the world so hungry that God
cannot appear to them except in the form of bread.

—Mahatma Gandhi

Lughnasadh, also known as Lammas, or "loaf mass," is the third festival on the light half of the wheel. Typically celebrated August 1, Lughnasadh is the first true autumn harvest festival of the year. However, before we get comfortable with the concept of a general harvest season celebration, Lughnasadh is not just any harvest festival; it is literally a wheat harvest, and the loaves are literally bread.

Lammas is the midpoint celebration between the summer solstice and the autumn equinox. Over time, this August 1 date has shifted a bit, and Lammas can be found to be celebrated anytime between August 1 through the first weekend after August 1. Lughnasadh is the last of the four Gaelic festivals, after Samhain, Imbolc, and Beltane. Lughnasadh has obvious Celtic origins, being named after the god Lugh. Lughnasadh comes from the old Irish name Lughnasad, which roughly translates to *Lugh* (the god) and *nasad* (assembly). While this version of the festival has an Irish origin, the modern Irish spelling of the festival is Lunasa, which is the month of August.

It is believed that Lughnasadh is the name for the festival of games that were established to honor the mother of the Celtic sun god Lugh. In *Celebrating the Seasons of Life: Beltane to Mabon*, Ashleen O'Gaea tells us that there were often games of speed and strength to show remaining vitality that would soon begin to die in harvest. It was understood that even in death, the circle of life will continue as we are nourished by the death of the harvest.

The concept of a wheat harvest holiday and the use of the word *sacrifice* shouldn't be lost on you. This concept may feel reminiscent of another popular god who is said to have sacrificed himself for humankind. However, there is no true relation between the two gods. For pagan gods, there is no element of "sin" or saving, but an exchange of energy in an ever-flowing cycle. The offering of bread to harvest and imminent death of our god are not so centered around us but rather part of the natural order and exchange of spiritual energy that flows through everything.

What is interesting about this day specifically is that there are a few different versions of the festival with all different players. In Ireland, we saw Lughnasadh and a festival centered around the god Lugh. In England, we saw the festival known as Lammas, aka loaf mass. Honestly, there is not a much better festival than one centered so squarely around carbs in a folk setting.

Going back to the origin of the wheel of the year, we remember that most Wiccan sabbats were taken from Celtic origins. Lughnasadh is no different, being Irish in origin. Unless you look at the Scottish, Welsh, or English versions. That is what makes Lammas so unique; each of these cultures, so closely related, had its own festival with similar yet unique traditions. What we see today in modern paganism is really a combination of every festival and the flavor of modern practice.

Lammas, Wheat, and the French Revolution

Lammas is the festival that marks the first wheat harvest. Additionally, it also happens to be the first harvest festival of the year and the first autumnal harvest as well. In some places, Lammas also marks the end of the hay harvest season. It should be noted that while Lammas and Lughnasadh start on the same day, originated in similar geographic areas, and have general theme overlaps, they are not in fact the same event.

Whereas Lughnasadh features both the veneration of the god Lugh and the wheat harvest, Lammas is more secular, focusing on general gods and the wheat harvest.

Historically, wheat has been one of the most important commodity and trade items in the world, and especially in Europe. Bread and other wheat products have been an important part in feeding people for generations, and during times of bad crop there have been full political uprisings.

In July 1789, the Bastille was stormed and the accessibility to bread may or may not have played a huge role in this (and the entire French Revolution). During the time of the Little Ice Age, crops were blighted in a serious manner. This led to a shortage of grain, specifically wheat. As the Little Ice Age continued, food shortages increased, and the availability of affordable food decreased.

In 1775, over three hundred riots were recorded stemming from an outrage over rising grain prices and availability of grain in general. This wave of protest was later called the Flour War and can feel reminiscent of some American revolutionary events. Grain products were especially important in France during this time period, because it is estimated that bread probably accounted for upward of 80 percent of the middle- and lower-class diet. Any change in availability or pricing sparked more than just unrest.

BRING ME THE DOUGH:
THOR'S DAY WHOLE WHEAT ALTAR BREAD

What better way to work with wheat than getting your hands down and dirty in it? I have been making and teaching this basic bread for prosperity for a few years, and each rendition of the bread gets better. This recipe was originally adapted from one that I found on the internet written by Nita Crabb.

Making your own altar bread, especially during a wheat harvest festival, connects you to the energy of your spiritual practice as well as shows your reverence and dedication to the gods and spirits you are observing.

This recipe makes two loaves. Leave one loaf on your altar and eat the other on the morning beginning Lughnasadh.

INGREDIENTS

- 3 cups warm water (110 degrees)
- 2 packages active dry yeast (0.25 ounces each)
- 2 tablespoons honey, plus 1/3 cup honey
- 5 cups white bread flour
- 1/2 cup oatmeal
- 1/2 cup dried cherries
- 1/2 cup raisins
- 3 tablespoons butter, melted
- 1 tablespoon salt
- 3 1/2 cups whole wheat flour

Preheat oven to 200 degrees. In a large bowl, mix warm water, yeast, and honey. Let stand for 5 minutes. Add white bread flour, oatmeal, cherries, and raisins and stir to combine. Let dough sit for 30 minutes, or until big and bubbly. Mix in melted butter, honey, and salt. Stir in 2 cups whole wheat flour.

If you have a stand-up mixer, mix using the dough hook until dough pulls away from sides of mixing bowl. If you do not have a mixer or prefer to knead by hand, flour a flat surface and knead with whole wheat flour until the dough is just barely pulling away from the counter. This may take an additional 1 to 2 cups of whole wheat flour; use discretion.

Once the dough has been kneaded, split it into two equal pieces. These are your two loaves.

Take the first piece, and separate it into three equal parts. Roll each section into a long, thick strand for braiding. As you braid the three strands together, thank the gods, universe, and your ancestors for your health, wealth, and prosperity. Each plat should have a thanksgiving attached to it.

Repeat the braiding process with the second loaf.

Place the loaves in a greased baking pan or dish and let rise in a warm oven for about 20 minutes. The loaves should double in size.

Once bread has risen, turn the oven to 350 degrees and set the timer for 25 minutes.

When the bread is golden brown, remove it from the oven and spread butter all over the warm loaves. Let cool for several minutes before removing from pan.

Take this simple cooking ritual up to the next level by also making butter to go with it. This bread is best made and eaten on Thursday or Sunday. Thursday is the day of Thor, and Sunday is the day of the sun. As Lugh is a sun god, and Lughnasadh is his harvest holiday, you could easily make this for any purpose. The wheat and the honey are meant to welcome in prosperity to the hearth and home.

GODDESS BUTTER RITUAL

Butter is considered sacred in many cultures and especially important in the Celtic-influenced cultures. Choosing to create butter will merge the energy of the God and the Goddess, welcoming them both into the harvest celebration that your body will partake in. Creating an altar meal for prosperity also shows our gods, guides, and ancestors that we value their presence and will ultimately further strengthen our relationships with them. By creating with cream, we can tap into its abundant energy and offer to the old gods.

This butter is a whole ritual related to manifesting prosperity and abundance, with the Goddess as our beacon of light. If you work with any specific goddess, feel free to call upon her when creating this butter. If you do not work with any specific goddesses, you can call upon Mother Nature, the lady of the land, your guides, your ancestors, or anyone you feel comfortable with.

Cream is typically associated with female deities because it is the life-sustaining source that females create for their offspring, but if you associate with nonbinary or male gods you can call upon them as well.

INGREDIENTS

For the altar:

- **Paper money of highest denomination you feel comfortable with**
- **Fresh basil leaves**
- **1 cinnamon stick**
- **Small piece of string**
- **1 green or yellow chime candle**

For the butter:

- **24 ounces heavy cream**
- **Pinch of sugar**
- **Pinch of salt**
- **Dried Italian seasoning (or dried basil) to taste (this has all the herbs you need for prosperity)**

To begin, take the paper money and fresh basil and roll them together with the cinnamon stick; the cinnamon stick should be in the middle. Tie this together with a piece of string and set it on your altar. In this working, basil is used to attract prosperity, while cinnamon is used to aid its speed and progress.

Next to this bundle, light your chime candle and welcome in your higher powers. Chime candles are small candles that can burn all the way down in one sitting, typically in less than 30 minutes, which is why they are useful when you are cooking.

Move over to your kitchen, and wash your hands in preparation to make the butter. In a large bowl or stand mixer add the heavy cream, sugar, salt, and Italian seasoning.

Mix on medium high for 15 to 20 minutes, until the butter separates from the liquid. This liquid portion is buttermilk, and you can save it for a future use.

Take the butter in your hands and squeeze out the remainder of the milk. (This is important!) I keep a second bowl of ice water while I do this because I find that it helps extract the milk.

Place the butter into a bowl or jar, and set it next to your bread and candle on the altar. Give thanks to your guides, ancestors, and higher powers, and invite them to enjoy. If you intend to make enough butter for personal use, fresh butter will keep about two weeks refrigerated.

16

MABON

[september 21–23
harvest home, harvest end, autumn equinox
fourth spoke on the dark side of the modern wheel of the year]

Autumn is a second spring, when every leaf is a flower.

—Albert Camus

Mabon is the name given to the autumn equinox. The autumn equinox is the second harvest festival of the three harvest festivals in the pagan wheel of the year, and it typically falls between September 21 and September 23. The autumn equinox divides the daytime and nighttime equally, which allows us to take a pause before we are overrun with the darkness of winter.

Mabon is considered one of the lesser observances on the wheel of the year, but it is also one of my favorites. It is the last festival in the light half of the wheel and thought to be named after the Celtic Welsh god Mabon. Mabon is a god of light and was the son of the earth mother goddess Modron ("mother").

In Lughnasadh, we watched as the God acknowledged his final decline before the cycle of death and rebirth. Mabon is a time when death is upon us. It is not as solemn as it seems, though, because we know he will be reborn during your time. This is the cycle, as it has been and as it always will be.

As the second harvest festival, it's the time for joy and celebrating the fruits of one's labor. Alongside Mabon are the separate celebrations of Harvest End and Harvest Home. Harvest End and Harvest Home were times for the gathering of the last harvest and a celebration of abundance. A traditional English harvest festival, Harvest Home is celebrated today on the last day of September, when towns are decorated and corn dollies are made to represent the spirits of the field.

The God Mabon

Mabon is the name of a Celtic god, and the son of Modron, who was the great mother. Similar to Demeter and Persephone, Modron mourned the loss of Mabon after he was abducted three days after his birth. Mabon was imprisoned inside of a stone wall, but was later released.

It's interesting how two separate cultures have created similar stories where a god or goddess was for some reason taken away from the earth against their will. In their absence, winter falls on the earth, freezing everything in its path. This is, of course, the cycle of life—but it is interesting how similar stories persist across various parts of Europe.

Michaelmas

The equinox was converted to a feast day in the Catholic Church. Michaelmas, also known as the Feast of Saint Michael and All Angels, is celebrated and observed on September 29. This day is considered a "quarter day," along with the spring equinox and the two solstices.

Saint Michael is not a traditional saint, but an angel. There are many witches who choose to work with Judeo-Christian angels, so for those who do, acknowledging this feast day would be relevant to their spiritual practice. In many folk practices, there are witches who choose to continue working with Abrahamic concepts after they excommunicate themselves from the religion as a whole. To them, being a pagan or witch doesn't necessitate the thought that those concepts of angels, saints, etc., are off limits or in any way no longer valid. For example, according to Jake Richards, author of *Backwoods Witchcraft*, Appalachian folk magick practitioners often use the Christian Bible as a sort of spellbook.

Saint Michael is the leader of all the angels in the army of God. According to scripture and tradition, Saint Michael has four responsibilities: combating Satan, escorting the faithful to heaven at the time of their death, championing Christians and the Church, and calling men to their judgment.

As the year turns again and again from light to dark, the celebration of Michaelmas took hold throughout the British Isles as a way to encourage protection during the cold and dark winter months. There is a proverb that goes, "Eat a goose on Michaelmas Day, want not for money all the year." Being as how Mabon doesn't have many traditions directly associated with it, this is a suggestion that could easily be adopted. It is thought that this proverb originated from Queen Elizabeth I. When she heard news of the defeat of the Spanish Armada, she was dining on goose and decided that she would partake in it every Michaelmas Day from that point forward.

Lilith's Apple

When I was fifteen, I was given a lovely vintage book called *The Complete Old Wives' Lore for Gardeners* by Bridget and Maureen Boland. It was decorated throughout with woodcut prints and covered so many things, from literal garden lore to basic (unintentional) witchcraft practices to actual useful gardening tips. Nothing, however, stuck with me as much as a little paragraph about the protection offered by apple trees:

> *When an apple [tree] is planted the name of Asmodeus, the devil who tempted Eve (unless you believe it was the she-devil, Lilith), should be written on the earth and cancelled with a cross.*

Throughout my life, I've planted quite a few apple trees and have always remembered this basic ritual. Apples have a rich magickal lore, being a major part of the harvest season. Instead of banishing Lilith, as is common in many texts, we will call on her for fertility, protection, and guidance. Apples are an abundant, fertile fruit that will bless you over again with love magick, prosperity magick, baneful magick, and pretty much everything in between.

Due to the incoming weather, the autumn equinox is not the best time to plant an apple tree; however, it is a great time to partake in apple picking or make candied apples. During autumn apples are abundant and can be used anytime to invoke and welcome the intelligence and protection of Lilith.

AN APPLE A DAY

One of my absolute favorite parts about fall (as if I could pick just one) is apple picking. There is something about driving out to an apple orchard, picking apples from old trees, getting cider and fresh apple cinnamon donuts that just automatically bumps the experience up way past what any other season can offer. Stolen from my childhood (we don't have apple orchards in South Florida), apple picking is something I fell dearly in love with when I moved to New England. In terms of witchcraft, apples have a wide range of talents they can lend themselves to. Apples can help bring in prosperity, their seeds can be used for protection, and they can be used as an offering during the harvest months. If cut in half horizontally, the seeds often form a pentacle shape.

The only drawback about apple picking is that I always pick too much! I *live* for the experience, and I get too excited, honestly. My friends tend to make fun of me, but when you do something for the first time as an adult, you have to make up for lost time. Coming home with all these apples in the fall had me wondering what on earth I could do with them. The obvious answer (to me) was to make a pie. But there were still some left over after the pie.

Enter: apple candle holders! I am not the inventor of this idea, as I'm sure people have been doing it for as long as there have been apples and candles. But what I can say is that these candle holders make the most beautiful Mabon altar decorations and can be used inside and outside.

You will need:

- **Red apples (because they look the best and tend to be sweeter)**
- **Taper or tealight candle**
- **Sharpie**
- **Paring knife**
- **Lemon juice**

Holding your candle to an apple, take your Sharpie and mark where you want it to go. With your paring knife, carve out the place where the candle will fit. Once the top part has been removed, put some lemon juice on the apple to keep it from browning. If using a taper, let it dry a little bit and then drip some wax in the apple to secure the candle in place. If using a tealight candle, drop it in and enjoy your new candle holder. These candle holders can last up to a few days.

17

THE NONTRADITIONAL YEAR

*They always say time changes things,
but you actually have to change them yourself.*

—Andy Warhol

The neopagan wheel of the year is comfortable. It's beloved to many, and observed quite literally eight times a year. It has festivals from various cultures, themes that have the potential to feel like home. And yet, it didn't always seem that way to me. This is something I have personally struggled with and come back to time and time again as a pagan. What does it mean to be connected to the wheel of the year if the wheel of the year isn't connected to me?

It makes sense when you think about it—the wheel of the year as we know it was made in England. I currently live in the tropics. Prior to this, I lived in an area of Montana that has a climate classification of "continental subarctic," which means that on average it only has fifty to ninety days in the whole year with an average temperature of 63 degrees. Having lived in two polar extremes in terms of climate and temperature has left me feeling really misplaced amid the wheel of the year. People were watching leaves fall while I was either snowed in or on a beach. Something had to give!

All over the world, there are pagans and witches living in places that do not align with the wheel of the year. These are places that do not follow four set seasons, and sometimes don't even follow the seasons they are supposed to. For example, Death Valley in the Southwest averages just two inches of rainfall per year! There are countless examples of unique climates across the country and the planet, and learning how to work with them, versus against them, will allow us to enjoy practicing the wheel of the year again!

A Brief Overview of the Wheel of the Year

There are lots of terms for the wheel of the year, and sometimes it can get confusing. Knowing the ins and outs of the wheel is what will lay the foundations for us to change it to suit our needs, so it is important to go over some of the basics. The wheel of the year is comprised of eight sabbats, or holidays. The eight sabbats of the wheel of the year are comprised of four quarter dates, and four cross-quarter dates. One notable difference between quarter days and cross-quarter days is that quarter days move, whereas cross-quarter days are (nearly) fixed. Quarter days include the spring and fall equinox and the winter and summer solstice. Cross-quarter days are the Celtic fire festivals that fall halfway between the quarter days: Samhain, Imbolc, Beltane, and Lughnasadh.

The eight sabbats of the wheel of the year are, once again:

- Samhain / Halloween: October 31 / November 1
- Yule: winter solstice
- Imbolc: February 1
- Ostara: spring equinox
- Beltane: May 1
- Litha / Midsummer: summer solstice
- Lughnasadh: August 1
- Mabon: fall equinox

Wheel of the Problems

These sabbats seem pretty universal, right? We all get a solstice and an equinox, after all! While this is true and every pagan experiences these celestial events, not every pagan experiences the wheel of the year as it is written. For example Yule, the winter solstice, is hallmarked with winter lore—it *is* a winter festival! To witches who live anywhere in the world where it does not snow, connecting to the specific lore of a Germanic holiday becomes difficult, if not somewhat painful.

Each sabbat on the wheel of the year has similar issues. Outside of fairly specific climates (western Europe, New England, etc.), the wheel of the year really doesn't make much sense. I can connect with an equinox; however, I am unable to connect with the fall themes surrounding the equinox. In a world where everyone enjoys showcasing their spiritual practice to an online audience, this can create a lot of guilt in witches who think maybe they're not doing enough when in reality they are just not being called to connect to the wheel of the year the way it was written for Wiccans.

This may be something that you haven't heard before, so let me say it loudly—it is okay to change the wheel of the year in your personal practice. It should be *expected* and *encouraged* for you to take initiative to connect to the earth in your earth-based religion. My personal wheel of the year observes twelve degrees split between two halves, instead of the traditional eight. I chose to split my wheel of the year up into months because I feel it gives me a better grasp on what is happening and allows me to really *see* the earth where I am right now.

Additionally, choosing to split up my wheel of the year has allowed me to let it travel wherever I go. The first flower of spring is never announced with loud fanfare, but it breaks through the ground all the same. Celebrating the energy of the earth, in my opinion, shouldn't be delegated to just a few specific days. These sabbats do find a home on my wheel of the year, but they are not the focus of my year.

Instead, my wheel of the year has become a year of the witch—something that supports me and my journey through earth-based paganism. I went through many years (nearly my whole time as a witch, actually) without any gods and chose to instead focus on the local spirits that surrounded my area and interacted with me daily. This looked like making star fruit wine after a particularly good harvest season and sharing it around a bonfire with friends. It also looks like making every harvest and super moon something to be celebrated and revered. Harvest moons indicate a change of the season, a time to celebrate as we turn into the next spoke on the wheel of the year. In the next chapter, we will go over in better detail ways to look at the wheel of the year and customize it for your specific path!

Down South

Because of the seasons being so different in the southern hemisphere, it begs the question of how to observe the wheel of the year there. In general, there are two types of solutions for this problem. Some people believe that the pagan holidays in the wheel of the year should be celebrated as the original cultures intended them to be. For example, Yule would be celebrated in December regardless of what hemisphere you're in. You would still bring into your tree, and you would still decorate it regardless of whether it is winter or summer outside.

The second camp of thought is that paganism is a nature-based spiritual practice. This means that to practice the religion and spirituality, you only have to follow nature. Since nature is in summer where you are, you would celebrate the summer holidays instead of the winter holidays.

There's not really a good solution here. In my opinion, it would be up to the individual witch to decide how they are going to celebrate the wheel of the year. If it is important to them to observe cultural traditions with the wheel of the year, then those witches would probably observe the festivals in the same way as someone in the northern hemisphere would. Because to them, the festival is as much about the culture that created it as the festival is itself. Others though, would prefer to celebrate the cycles and seasons and harvests as they are where they live.

There really is no right or wrong answer here—it is just personal preference. No matter which hemisphere you live in, you're going to experience winter and summer solstice and spring and autumn equinox. You're also going to experience your own unique harvest cycles.

So how do you celebrate a winter holiday during the summer months? Perhaps you don't! Listen to the earth around you, feel its energy. As you acknowledge and celebrate the changes on the other side of the world, remember to carve out a little space to appreciate and revere where you are right now.

18

CREATING YOUR OWN WHEEL

Others have seen what is and asked why
I have seen what could be and asked why not.

—Pablo Picasso

Creativity strikes us when we are least expecting it! If you'd have told me when I was first starting out that I would be drastically deviating from the neopagan wheel of the year I first learned, I would have called you a liar. I mean, that's *the wheel of the year*. But when the universe calls, it's important to slow down and listen.

Growing up, my family celebrated nearly any festival, holiday, and holy day that was printed on a calendar. My mom payed extra attention to saint feast days, and her favorite holidays were Christmas and Halloween (in that order). The decorations for any holiday would come out weeks in advance, and she would cook themed dinners. Still to this day I find myself traumatized after one particular Halloween when she decided to throw a "haunted house" in our driveway. She cooked spaghetti and put it in the fridge to cool. There was also a bowl of eyes, which I think may have been small hard-boiled eggs (or maybe peeled grapes?). All I know is that I ran screaming from my own house after my mother made me stick my hand in a bowl of spaghetti brains.

A few years back, I really started to analyze myself, my spirituality, why I did the things I did and believed in certain things. One of the elements I looked at the hardest was the wheel of the year. It didn't *fit*. Was I still obligated to use it to be a pagan or a witch? The answer is a resounding NO. This wheel was only created a little over sixty years ago, and you can deviate from it as much or as little as you'd like and still be a "real witch."

When the English Wiccans decided to put their calendar together, they sourced most of their holidays from the Irish, Scottish, Welsh, and Germanic peoples. Not only did they take these holidays out of their original context with the original gods, but they gave no credit to the cultures and origins of the festivals, leaving many gaps in practice. It's taken many years for the wider pagan community to unravel the wheel and gain insight into the origins of the festivals.

There is one huge secret in modern paganism: you don't actually have to celebrate the festivals at the same time everyone else does. I personally don't celebrate most of the harvest festivals when the rest of the world does, because it doesn't make sense for the climate I live in. August 1 is the wheat harvest festival Lammas or Lughnasadh. South Florida is hot as hell in early August. We're not harvesting wheat here, and we certainly aren't baking bread. So this holiday is basically excluded from my wheel. Sometimes I do acknowledge it if I'm on vacation up north because it's fun, but otherwise it's not really a part of my practice.

The wheel you create is as flexible as you are! Some religious and spiritual holidays aren't superflexible—and celestial events aren't, either. (The solstice will always be on the solstice.) However, you get the freedom to choose when and how you will observe these traditions in your own practice. The wheel is ever turning, and it is as malleable as you are. Just because you decide something about your wheel today doesn't mean that you can't adjust it at a later date if need be.

When we first start building our wheel of the year and actually using it, it is really important to keep a written record. What festivals and celebrations have you partaken in, and would you do them again? Which parts were superfun and what made them so? Was it the schedule of events? The rituals you performed? The people you celebrated with? All of the above?

As we go through life, we are constantly taking in new information and shifting the way we handle things. If you discover new gods/goddesses along the way, or end up finding out things about your ancestry you didn't know previously, you're able to incorporate those elements into your wheel without much stress! When you move to a new place, you can either shift or create a whole new wheel that fits your new climate and routine. This allows you to have freedom not only in your practice but also in your personal life.

There are tons of pagan holidays outside of the eight that were picked to be on the wheel of the year. The exhaustive source *Religious Holidays and Calendars* lists thirty-one *pagan* holidays, not to mention tons of other festivals and holidays from any of the other religions. When you are creating your wheel, you are master of your ship. If you want to incorporate religious holidays from your culture, there is literally nothing that prevents you from doing that. Part of the reason that my wheel has twelve points instead of eight was so that I could incorporate other religious holy days into my wheel.

The best way to start creating your own wheel is to get a little crafty. Similar to how you might make a mood board (or a Pinterest board), you're going to make a board for your wheel of the year. You'll need some pictures, paper, scissors, and glue. I find that doing this by hand, rather than digitally, makes it feel more real when it comes time to actually build the wheel.

Starting with January, write down all of your thoughts related to that month. Then proceed through all the rest of the months.

Here's an example of what my list looks like, living in warm, humid South Florida:

January: mild weather, beaches, Art Deco festival, Valencia orange
season begins
February: man-of-war fish, cool weather, food and wine, strawberry
picking
March: Irish music, overcast, rainy, Miami Carnival, melon season
begins

April: bright sunshine, hot but not humid, my birthday, tax time, blueberry season begins

May: hot, stressed, sun is bright but not obnoxious, mango season begins

June: rainy, hot, humid, avocado season begins

July: hot, humid, rainy, watermelon, good sunlight, plants can get injured in afternoon sun, fireworks, passion fruit season begins

August: hot, humid, don't go outside, grape season begins, Cotton Candy grapes at Publix

September: pre-Halloween, good afternoon sun, hot, squash season begins, tomatoes are growing

October: Halloween season, best light, books, navel orange season begins

November: daylight saving time, best light, early sunsets, dragonfruit season ends

December: cool, dry, blue-toned light, pomelo season begins

Once you've completed your list, add what you consider to be spiritual elements for each of the months. Below is an example of how I personally see the year, based on where I live and my personal life experience. I also like to assign an element that I relate to each month to make it easier to create spellwork and rituals. These elements change and shift through time, and location. I would expect that your elemental choices will look different than mine. Not only do I want that, I encourage you to make your own connections and truly take the reins in creating a wheel that works for you and your magick.

I tend to really notice the lighting during the year. It's not overcast where I live, it's not cold, there's no snow, and there's no death. There is literally no dormant season in Florida, and if anything, our winter is our most productive season. This is a time when you get to go through all of the holidays and festivals and see which ones align with how you view the year. Create a separate list in the same way as your spiritual notes and thoughts for the months of the year (here is mine for example):

January	calm, quiet, restful	*air*
February	chaotic, energetic, fast-paced, love	*water*
March	home, melancholic	*water*
April	warm, lust, birth	*fire*
May	stagnant, on the cusp	*earth*
June:	falling, movement without direction	*water*
July	procrastination, changes, working through problems	*fire*
August	motivation, a new beginning	*fire*
September	motivation and change, heavy, falling	*air*
October:	the end, death, destruction, quiet	*fire*
November:	peaceful, rushed, meditative	*earth*
December	calm, hopeful, rumination	*earth*

Last, take note of any particular cultural traditions and established festivals you might want to incorporate. These can be secular, religious, spiritual, or even family-bound. If you want to hold a spiritual observance on September 11 every year as part of your calendar, you have the freedom to do so. Days of large-scale remembrance often come with a thinning of the veil, and I have no doubt that over time the American people have worn their veil thin on that day. Family events that may be added to your year of the witch can include birthdays, anniversaries, death days, recovery markers, etc. These days hold personal significance and when added to our wheels, allow us to maintain connections with our emotional needs as well as our spiritual ones.

Merging these ideas and concepts into one fluid wheel is the most exciting part of your craft. It does away with the pressure of doing things the "right" way when you first start. Creating a system that works for you allows the energy of your spirit and your ancestors' spirits to flow freely. Remember those pictures and magazines I talked about earlier? It's time to create a mood board. For each month, take a look at what you've described above. What are the characteristics you associate with each month? What do those characteristics look like? Give yourself free range to create a collage for each month. Use words, pictures, and your intuition to create your own piece of the year!

Taking a look at my wheel (in written form below), you can see that some of the modern pagan celebrations are not here: specifically Lughnasadh and Imbolc. To me, neither of these festivals really aligns with the nature I experience in a daily basis. Additionally, I observe three harvests specific to my climate: mango harvest, avocado harvest, and orange harvest. I have a mix of secular and religious holidays, and I observe the changing of hurricane season and "normal" season as my primary method of organization. My wheel also isn't a "circle," but more of a tiered priority system. This is the wheel that works for me where I am in my life physically, mentally, and spiritually. Your chart will no doubt look different. Have fun filling it in and deciding when and how you want to celebrate it. Remember: there is no wrong way to be yourself!

TEMPERANCE'S WHEEL OF THE YEAR

Hurricane Season *(June 1–November 30)*

Avocado Harvest *(May–June)*

Mango Harvest *(May–August)*

Litha *(summer solstice)*

Mabon *(autumn equinox)*

Days of Mourning *(September)*

Yom Kippur *(September–October)*

Samhain *(October–November)*

Orange Harvest *(November–April)*

Not Hurricane Season *(December 1–May 30)*

Orange Harvest *(November–April)*

Yule *(winter solstice)*

Saint Valentine's Day *(February 14)*

Ostara *(spring equinox)*

My Birthday *(April)*

Shark Season *(April)*

Beltane *(May 1)*

After looking at my wheel, take a second to really evaluate the holidays that you plan to work with. Where do they fit in? Do they have their own independence, or are they tied to a larger season, like how mine are all tied to hurricane season? Hurricane season is a time of year with increased rainfall, so I like to pay reverence to the coming storm season.

If your wheel could look like anything, what would you have on it?

Creating New Seasonal Traditions

The last part of creating and crafting your own wheel of the year is creating seasonal traditions that you not only observe but fully invest in and pass down! When I was first married, I spent the Yule season at my in-laws' house. Every night, my mother-in-law sat down in front of the TV and created a beautiful needlepoint Christmas ornament. As it turns out, she had made one for every year that she had been married. The ornaments were all themed and reflected a major life event within their marriage or lives.

When I asked her about why she did this, she told me that when she was first married, she was given a book of traditions to start a new family. There were three that she kept, including the needlepointed ornaments, Thanksgiving Day bread, and Christmas bread. As a result of starting these new traditions, all of her children now incorporate them as well. Her daughters are all married, and each of them has started a family needlepoint ornament collection. Additionally, every child has learned the recipes for Thanksgiving Day bread and Christmas bread. Watching these traditions start in one generation and be passed down two generations showed me a level of stability and love that I hadn't experienced before. Passing down traditions from one generation to the next is how the love of all of our ancestors survives.

When you start a new family tradition, it can be as simple as saying, "We eat fresh baked bread on Lammas," or as complex as taking twenty-five days to hand stitch an ornament for the Yule tree. The biggest catalyst for creating traditions and practices surrounding the wheel of the year was when I became pregnant. I had been living outside of the boundaries of "family" for over ten years at that point, having been orphaned as a child. I began to evaluate traditions and their importance to me and my growing family. What were things that I had done as a child that I could revamp now?

To me, the wheel of the year starts on Samhain, so that is where I started looking. I revived the family version of a dumb supper that I grew up knowing and loving. I moved into the orange harvest season next, which I have enjoyed incorporating into my yearly devotions. Where the north has apple picking, Florida has citrus U-Pick. Taking home bags of fresh oranges has its benefits—Pomander altar balls! Pomander balls are oranges that are covered with cloves in a decorative pattern. They are typically associated with the Yuletide season, and having picked them in November means I can make Pomander balls with my daughter for our seasonal altar to last through the season.

Growing up, Yuletide became a time when the hearth took priority in my home. If there weren't cookies in the oven, there was a pie or a cake. Nights were spent as a family watching old Christmas movies and reading books together. The value of Yuletide became presence—not presents.

Moving into the new calendar year, we observe the feast of Saint Valentine by cooking meals at home for each other.

During Ostara I drag my family and friends down to the local plant nursery to pick out the plants we want to grow through midsummer, and I'll occasionally pick up seeds for fall too. Planting seedlings in the garden allows for smaller children to be excited about creating and maintaining a small piece of the earth.

In April we celebrate birthdays, and welcome sharks to our waters. Sharks are a critical piece to the South Florida ocean life cycle, and I pray for their safety away from poachers. As the cycle starts again, I like to go to the beach and pick up trash that would otherwise end up in the ocean. I am devoted to a sea god, so I give my time in acts of service to try to help the health of my local waterways.

Each part of the wheel of the year has something small but significant that I do to reaffirm my devotion to my path. Being in ritual mode 24/7 isn't a sustainable or authentic practice for me, personally. I find that I am much more spiritually productive when I get time to be outside in nature creating and healing. Envision yourself during a harvest or holiday season when you want to start a tradition. What are you doing, and who is with you?

FINAL THOUGHTS

As I wind down in writing, I think it's fair to say the true work has just begun! Your wheel of the year starts here, and it starts right now. How we use the opportunities that we are given to positively change the world matter. What would happen to your practice if you were forced to move tomorrow? Would you be able to support your craft in a new setting with different lands, spirits, elements, and climates? Or would you find yourself struggling like a fish out of water, trying to connect using methods that are no longer effective for where you are?

A connected wheel of the year practice is extremely grassroots in that it encourages you to become one with the land you are on, to touch and experience everything that the earth has to offer you while staying grounded to the only constant that there is: time. It doesn't matter if you build a fancy aesthetic altar or prefer to get your daily dose of spirituality outdoors—what matters is that you take the time every day to push yourself and grow deeper in your craft. We are the only ones who are responsible for how far we go on the pathway that we walk.

It is surreal to be finishing this book, having written and struggled over every word in it. However, I think that it is increasingly important to have perspective from new voices on every topic in the witchcraft, pagan, and new age umbrella. I was approached recently by a woman who felt as though she needed to tell me that new witchcraft books are not worth buying. Her thought was that if you have read it before, you don't need to read it again. What more could you learn on candle magick, or water witchcraft, or the wheel of the year? How many books need to come out that say "the same thing"? But I think that opinion is rooted in ignorance.

There will always be something new to bring to the table in the world of spirituality. Each person has a unique and divine connection to the universe that makes their narrative special. My narrative has been learning how to navigate and love the wheel of the year, even when I want to dislike it or feel constrained by it. It is my perspective that melds bits of science with bits of history and narrative that is uniquely my own.

So, quietly, this book concludes. The wheel of the year keeps turning, the sun will keep growing in the sky, heavy with possibility. Then it will recede and all but vanish. And then, just when we think all is lost, it will start again and we will know we are found in our place among nature. We as witches will rejoin nature not as masters of it, but as defenders and champions. Where will you be?

APPENDIX A

LIST OF PAGAN HOLIDAYS

This list does not include every pagan event or festival, but encompasses some of the more common ones celebrated by pagans around the world. It also includes holidays from Celtic, Germanic, Roman, Afro-Caribbean, Shinto, and folk cultures. There are a large number of folk witches and pagans who observe specific Catholic saint feast days, so I've included some of those as well.

OCTOBER

October 4

Feast Day of St. Francis of Assisi

Feast Day of Orula

October 31

Samhain Eve

NOVEMBER

November 1

Samhain

All Saint's Day

November 5

Guy Fawkes Night

November 11

Martinmas (Old Halloween)

DECEMBER

December 4

    Feast Day of St. Barbara

    Feast Day of Chango

December 17-23

    Saturnalia

Winter Solstice

    Yule (begins)

December 23

    Festivus

December 31

    Hogmany

    Omisoka

JANUARY

January 1

    New Year's Day

January 5

    Yule ends

FEBRUARY

February 1

    Imbolc

February 2

    Feast Day of Oya

February 3

    Setsubun

February 14

    Lupercalia

    Feast of St. Valentine

MARCH

March 3

    Hina Matsuri

Spring Equinox

    Feast for the Equinox Gods

    Ostara

    Shubun-sai

March 20

    Feast for the Supreme Ritual

March 22

    Feast Day of Orisha Oko

APRIL

April 8-10

    Feast for The Book of the Law

April 22

    Earth Day

April 30

    Walpurgis Night

MAY

May 1

    Beltane

    May Day

May 5

    Koi-no-bori

JUNE

June 6

    Feast Day of Ochosi

Summer Solstice

    Litha

June 24

    St. John the Baptist Day

June 29

    Feast Day of Ogun

June 30

Nagoshi-no-Oharai

JULY

July 13-15

Oban Festival

July 31

Lammas Eve

AUGUST

August 1

Lammas

Lughnasadh

August 12

Feast for the First Night of the Prophet and His Bride

August 13

Feast Day of Hekate

SEPTEMBER

September 7

Feast Day of Yemaya

September 8

Feast Day of Oshun

Fall Equinox

Mabon

Harvest Home

September 24

Feast Day of Our Lady of Mercy

Feast Day of Obatala

September 27

Feast Day of Ibeji

September 29

Feast Day of Erinle

Year of the Witch

APPENDIX B

CASCARILLA POWDER

Cascarilla powder is an easy-to-make essential ingredient for protective magick! Cascarilla (kas-ka-ree-ah) is made of powdered eggshell and used primarily for protection and spiritual cleansing. It originates from hoodoo and Santeria but has become popular throughout America due to its accessibility. Cascarilla powder can also help create spiritual barriers (similar to salt), add blessings, aid in protection, and is a great nutritional addition for plants in the garden!

White or brown eggshells can be used to make cascarilla powder, so just use whatever you have. If possible, it is easiest to have a bag under your sink or elsewhere in your kitchen to collect the eggshells over time.

Florida water (see Appendix C) is also known to have protective qualities and complements the cascarilla very well.

> **Pro tip:** When you crack an egg, run the shell under the kitchen faucet to separate the membrane from the shell. Removing the membrane makes a higher-quality powder.

Supplies:

- 2 dozen eggshells, dried
- Food processor or mortar and pestle
- ½ teaspoon Florida water
- Small glass jar / sealable container

Bake the eggshells at 200°F for approximately 30 minutes to further dry them out. This step allows excess moisture to cook off, making a finer powder. This step is especially important if you plan to grind the shells by hand using a mortar and pestle! If you are using white eggshells, you might notice the color change slightly. Don't worry—your powder will still come out white.

When the eggshells are done baking, grind them into a fine powder using a mortar and pestle or food processor. You will achieve a finer powder and save your muscles with a food processor. Add about ½ teaspoon of Florida water and process until you have a fine, sand-like consistency. Store the cascarilla powder in a jar or pack it into a chalk.

To make cascarilla chalk, mix 1 tablespoon of flour with 1 tablespoon of loose cascarilla powder and mix thoroughly. Add a tablespoon of warm water and mix until the ingredients have combined just enough to form a ball in your hands. Roll the mixture into sticks about ½ to 1 inch in diameter and let them dry for 3–5 days. Alternatively, you can roll the mixture into balls and place them in small paper condiment cups (this is the easiest method). Store the chalk in a glass, plastic, or metal container to protect it from breaking, and keep in a cool, dark place.

Note: You can enhance the magickal properties of your cascarilla powder by adding a small amount of powdered herbs to the mixture. You can add a dash of salt or ground rosemary for purification, a dash of ground cinnamon for protection, or a dash of ground cloves for money drawing. Just use caution when adding any of these—too much and the mixture will not stick together and form the chalk.

APPENDIX C

FLORIDA WATER

Florida water is a cologne used primarily to cleanse spaces and energy. Florida water is said to have gotten its name from two sources, one being the Fountain of Youth (said to exist in Florida) and the second being a translation of "floral" or "flowery." Florida water is fairly easy to DIY at home!

Supplies:
- 16 oz high proof vodka or rubbing alcohol
- Sprig of fresh rosemary
- 6 bay leaves (optional)
- ½ teaspoon clove essential oil
- ½ teaspoon lavender essential oil
- ½ teaspoon orange essential oil
- ¼ teaspoon vervain essential oil
- Smaller glass or plastic spray bottle

Pour approximately 1–2 ounces of the alcohol out of the container to create space to add ingredients to the bottle. Place the rosemary and bay leaves inside and shake gently to settle them. Add the essential oils and shake vigorously to combine. Store in a cool, dark place (a bookshelf or under a sink) and shake before each use. Transfer into smaller spray bottles to use for cleansing doorways, altars, cars, people, etc.

Acknowledgments

This book would not have been possible without the wonderful team at Weiser books for taking a chance. Big thank you to Peter, Christine, and Susie, who have been with me and supporting this wild journey through all of its turns.

Thank you to Kevin Marley and Nesi Smith, whose support on a personal level has meant the world to me and kept me going.

To Tim Heron, whose advice and thoughts on various topics really helped form a foundation for large sections of this book.

To Fiona, who absolutely did not want to let me write this book and would have preferred I watch ghostbusters with her instead. (At least they are interesting, she tells me.)

Thank you to Brandy, Stephanie, Micahaela, and Jorge for unknowingly being the most amazing friends when I wanted to give up. They say it takes a village to raise a child, but it *truly* takes a village to write a book!

Bibliography

Adler, Margot. *Drawing Down the Moon*. New York: Penguin, 1979.

Allen, Ginger M., and Martin B Main. *Florida's Geological History*. Department of Wildlife Ecology and Conservation, Florida Cooperative Extension Service, Institute of Food and Agricultural Sciences, University of Florida, 2005, *www.orange.wateratlas.usf.edu*.

Andrews, Ted. *Simplified Magic: A Beginner's Guide to the New Age Qabala*. St. Paul, MN: Llewellyn, 1989.

Auryn, Mat. *Psychic Witch: A Metaphysical Guide to Meditation, Magick & Manifestation*. Woodbury, MN: Llewellyn, 2020.

Baker, Jerry. *Jerry Baker's Old-Time Gardening Wisdom: Lessons Learned from Grandma Putt's Kitchen Cupboard, Medicine Cabinet, and Garden Shed!* New Hudson, MI: American Master Products, 2002.

Bartholomew, Mel. *Square Foot Gardening: A New Way to Garden in Less Space with Less Work*. New York: Rodale, 2005.

Bellenir, Karen, ed. *Religious Holidays and Calendars: An Encyclopedic Handbook*. Detroit, MI: Omnigraphics, 2009.

Blackthorn, Amy. *Sacred Smoke: Clear Away Negative Energies and Purify Body, Mind, and Spirit*. Newburyport, MA: Weiser Books, 2019.

Boland, Bridget, and Maureen Boland. *The Complete Old Wives' Lore for Gardeners*. London: The Bodley Head, 1989.

Borrero, Francisco J., et al. *Glencoe Earth Science: Geology, the Environment and the Universe*. Columbus, OH: McGraw-Hill, 2017.

Burton, Nylah. "Is Burning Sage Cultural Appropriation? Here's How to Smoke Cleanse in Sensitive Ways." *Bustle*, July 19, 2019, *www.bustle.com*

Campanelli, Pauline, and Dan Campanelli. *Wheel of the Year: Living the Magical Life*. Woodbury, MN: Llewellyn, 2003.

Campisano, Christopher. "Milankovitch Cycles, Paleoclimatic Change, and Hominin Evolution." *Nature Education Knowledge* 4, no. 3: 5.

Cavendish, Richard. *The Black Arts: A Concise History of Witchcraft, Demonology, Astrology, Alchemy, and Other Mystical Practices Throughout the Ages*. New York: Perigee, 2017.

Cicero, Chic, and Sandra Tabatha Cicero. *The Essential Golden Dawn: An Introduction to High Magic*. Woodbury, MN: Llewellyn, 2011.

Deerman, Dixie, and Steve Rasmussen. *The Goodly Spellbook: Olde Spells for Modern Problems*. New York: Sterling, 2005.

Ede-Weaving, Maria. "A Call to the Goddess and God of Imbolc." The Order of Bards, Ovates and Druids, *www.druidry.org*

Farrar, Janet, and Stewart Farrar. *The Witches Way: Principles, Rituals and Beliefs of Modern Witchcraft*. Blaine, WA: Phoenix Publishing, 1988.

Gardner, Gerald Brosseau. *Witchcraft Today*. New York, NY: Citadel Press, 1954.

Gary, Gemma. *The Black Toad: West Country Witchcraft and Magic*. Woodbury, MN: Llewellyn, 2020.

Gary, Gemma. *Traditional Witchcraft: A Cornish Book of Ways*. Woodbury, MN: Llewellyn, 2020.

Green, Marian. *Wild Witch: A Guide to Earth Magic*. Newburyport, MA: Weiser Books, 2019.

Heron, Dr. Timothy (ravenrunes). "Lightwork is Not the Same as Witchcraft," Instagram TV, *www.instagram.com*, December 2, 2019).

Herstik, Gabriela. *Inner Witch: A Modern Guide to the Ancient Craft*. New York: Perigee, 2018.

Hodgkinson, G. P., J. Langan-Fox, and E. Sadler-Smith. "Intuition: A Fundamental Bridging Construct in the Behavioural Sciences." *British Journal of Psychology* 99 (2008): 1–27.

Houghton, John. *Global Warming: The Complete Briefing*. Cambridge, United Kingdom: Cambridge University Press, 2009.

Howard, Michael. *The Sacred Ring: The Pagan Origins of British Folk Festivals and Customs*. Freshfields, Chieveley, Berks: Capall Bann, 1995.

Hutton, Ronald. *The Stations of the Sun: A History of the Ritual Year in Britain*. New York: Oxford University Press, 1996.

Kallestrup, Louise Nyholm. *Agents of Witchcraft in Early Modern Italy and Denmark*. New York: Palgrave Macmillan, 2015.

Koren, Marina. "The Pandemic Is Turning the Natural World Upside Down." *The Atlantic*, April 2, 2020, *www.theatlantic.com*.

Lazic, Tiffany. *The Great Work: Self-Knowledge and Healing Through the Wheel of the Year*. Woodbury, MN: Llewellyn, 2015.

Lewis, Rabbi Mendy. "Tzav: Our Internal and External Fires." *Jewish Standard*, April 6, 2017, *jewishstandard.timesofisrael.com*.

The Malleus Maleficarum of Heinrich Kramer and James Sprenger. Trans. Reverend Montague Summers. New York: Dover, 1971.

McIlvenna, Una. "How Bread Shortages Helped Ignite the French Revolution." History.com, A&E Television Networks, September 30, 2019, *www.history.com*.

Meredith, Jane. *Circle of Eight: Creating Magic for Your Place on Earth*. Woodbury, MN: Llewellyn, 2015.

Nock, Judy Ann. *The Modern Witchcraft Guide to the Wheel of the Year: From Samhain to Yule, Your Guide to the Wiccan Holidays*. Avon, MA: Adams Media, 2017.

O'Gaea, Ashleen. *Celebrating the Seasons of Life: Beltane to Mabon: Lore, Rituals, Activities, and Symbols*. Franklin Lakes, NJ: New Page Books, 2005.

O'Gaea, Ashleen. *Celebrating the Seasons of Life: Samhain to Ostara: Lore, Rituals, Activities, and Symbols.* Franklin Lakes, NJ: New Page Books, 2004.

Orchard, Brian. "Tied to the Land." Vision, Fall 2011, *www.vision.org.*

Rajchel, Diana. *Mabon: Rituals, Recipes and Lore for the Autumn Equinox.* Woodbury, MN: Llewellyn, 2015.

Richards, Jake. *Backwoods Witchcraft: Conjure and Folk Magic from Appalachia.* Newburyport, MA: Weiser Books, 2019.

Riebeek, Holli. "The Carbon Cycle." NASA, June 16, 2011, *earthobservatory.nasa.gov.*

Serith, Ceisiwr. *A Book of Pagan Prayer.* Newburyport, MA: Weiser Books, 2018.

Starhawk. *The Spiral Dance: A Rebirth of the Ancient Religion of the Great Goddess.* New York: HarperSanFrancisco, 1999.

Streep, Peg. *Spiritual Gardening: Creating Sacred Space Outdoors.* Makawao, HI: Inner Ocean, 2003.

Zotigh, Dennis. "Native Perspectives on the 40th Anniversary of the American Indian Religious Freedom Act." *Smithsonian Magazine*, November 30, 2018, *www.smithsonianmag.com.*

To Our Readers

Weiser Books, an imprint of Red Wheel/Weiser, publishes books across the entire spectrum of occult, esoteric, speculative, and New Age subjects. Our mission is to publish quality books that will make a difference in people's lives without advocating any one particular path or field of study. We value the integrity, originality, and depth of knowledge of our authors.

Our readers are our most important resource, and we appreciate your input, suggestions, and ideas about what you would like to see published.

Visit our website at *www.redwheelweiser.com* to learn about our upcoming books and free downloads, and be sure to go to *www.redwheelweiser.com/newsletter* to sign up for newsletters and exclusive offers.

You can also contact us at *info@rwwbooks.com* or at

Red Wheel/Weiser, LLC
65 Parker Street, Suite 7
Newburyport, MA 01950